THE DAILY STAND

A SPIRITUAL WARFARE INSTRUCTION MANUAL FOR TODAY AND THE UPCOMING NEXT GREAT MOVE OF GOD

Tom Snow

JUST TO BE CLEAR TEACHING SERIES

THE TRUTH THE LIGHT THE BLOOD

IN THE NAME OF JESUS

BARAK

Go To

https://just2beclear.com/stand-and-swim/

To sign up for Free Monthly

Newsletters, Gifts, and Discounts

T HIS MANUAL IS DEDICATED to the Lord Jesus Christ, the Holy Spirit, and Papa God, the Father.

I also dedicate this to my wonderful wife, Danielle, my perfect mate.

CONTENTS

NOTES

A LL VERSES OR FRAGMENTS of verses are taken from New American Standard Version Bible (NASV)®, New International Version Bible (NIV)®, The Amplified Bible (AMP)®, King James Version (KJV)®, or Strong's® Greek and Hebrew original texts and may be noted as such or not. All other names, trademarks, and any other such rights are owned by their respective originators. All other rights are reserved.

FOREWORD

For though we walk (live) in the flesh, we are not carrying on our warfare according to the flesh and using mere human weapons. For the weapons of our warfare are not physical [weapons of flesh and blood], But they are mighty before God for the overthrow and destruction of strongholds (or fortresses), [inasmuch as we] refute arguments, theories, speculations, reasonings, vain imaginations, and every proud, high, and lofty thing (or thought) that sets itself up against the [true] knowledge of God; And we lead every thought and purpose away captive into the obedience of Christ.

Second Corinthians 10:3–5 AMP

CHAPTER ONE

WHO I AM AND HOW I GOT HERE

HOW I CAME TO KNOW THE LORD

I was birthed in the early Charismatic movement.

I HAD CANCER

In 1969 to 1970, I was dying of cancer at age fifteen to sixteen years old—and I was afraid.

I was born a Jew—from both my father's and mother's sides—but did not know that lineage until later, so instead, I was raised in denominational (Presbyterian and Lutheran) churches. Nevertheless, I did not know the Lord.

Compounding my fears, my mother had just died the year previous from cancer and I blamed myself for her death. I was full of guilt. I felt shame. I was sad. I was terrified, yet I was torn.

When I found out I had cancer, I felt I DESERVED getting it and DESERVED to die—since I was carelessly doing experiments with large amounts of asbestos dust in the family home basement for my Science Fair project. In my preparation and studies, I "knew," yet "didn't take serious enough," the dangers of asbestos. I did it just so (in my fourteen-year-old ego) I could create a (stupid) new invention to win my State Science Fair—which I did. *SO WHAT!*

It wasn't worth hurting my mother (or me). But because of the guilt and shame, I never told anyone about the rock-hard tumor that I noticed growing in my abdomen—starting just one month after my mother's passing.

What I didn't know was there were deadly curses coming from both sides of the lineage against my mother (and my family)—first, from my father's mother, the "Jewish witch"—who was well-known and sought after because her curses always came true—who had cursed my mother to die an early painful death—which she did. And second, from my mother's father, the orthodox Rabbi, who sat rocking in a zombie-like trance chanting curses on her until the day he died.

You might ask why both people hated my mother so much to do these horrid things to her (and us). Fair question. But actually that is a vast story, spanning multiple generations, starting in the late 1800's—up through those years—and more. It would take another book to begin to explain all that's involved—maybe that could be my next book, called *Breaking the Curse of the Generations*—we'll see.

I know that sons love their mothers. But for the record, my mother was a wonderful, loving person—tough, but loving. A woman to be admired for many reasons.

So while my experiments didn't help the situation—they weren't the root cause of her death. I didn't know that, at that time, and not until many, many years later—all part of the same story.

Back to my situation. I had no hope. I didn't know where I was going when I died. The words "going to heaven" did not connect. I felt alone.

VISION OF CLOUDS OF TIME

During this time, I would come home from high school, sit in my family room, alone. My father was gone working long hours, and my two older brothers were away in college and the military, respectively.

For many months, I'd close my eyes and see the same vision in my mind—over and over, day after day. I'd look from one end of the horizon to the other and see a single series of cloud puffs just slowly moving along. On top of each cloud was a scene in time.

I would stare at the farthest cloud puff I could see, starting on the left where they began. I would watch it slowly move along until it got overhead, then I'd look at the scene on top. It was a scene in time of people and things living on—without me.

I'd watch that cloud puff until it reached the far end of the horizon, on the right, then I'd look back to the farthest cloud puff I could see on the left and do the same—over and over and over again.

It left me with a helpless feeling. Time was not going to stop when I died. That scared me— because I didn't know where I was going for eternity.

This happened nonstop every day with no end.

Then one day, while I was sitting there, watching the endless eternal progression of clouds, fearing the future, something very strange happened.

I heard the audible voice of the Lord.

YES!

I mean audible.

He said, "I love you" and "Someday, I'll provide your perfect mate for you." It came across, as loud as roaring thunder.

Nevertheless, it surrounded me with so much love—an overwhelming love I'd never felt before, anywhere, and so much of that love I could never question it.

It was like rivers of living waters, full of LOVE, flowing over me.

In John 7:37–39,

"Jesus stood, and said in a loud voice, 'If anyone is thirsty, let him come to Me and drink. He who believes in Me, as the Scripture said, from his innermost being will flow rivers of living water.' But this He spoke of the Spirit, whom those who believed in Him were to receive."

It was amazing!

He'd had answered two questions that plagued me.

One, I finally knew that God was real and near, not just some "faraway God who created the universe" but a true, living, and close Father who actually loved *Me—Me! UNBELIEVABLE!* And two, knowing I was dying—I was sure that I'd never get to know or enjoy the love of a mate and sex.

I was a fifteen to sixteen-year-old boy, so no doubt, yes, sex was on my mind. It was one of my big worries—other than dying.

The second part didn't make any sense since I was shortly doomed to be six feet under, so I ignored that part, but the first part echoed through my whole being!

But how could I get there? How could I reach the Father in time, before I died? How? How? How? Is all I could think.

BRUCE

Then one day, about a month later, my father and I were sitting together in the family room, watching TV when my brother, Bruce, came home from college and told us a "crazy" story.

Bruce proceeded to tell us that he had been on a bad LSD trip and called out on the Lord Jesus to save him. Jesus did and took him down off that trip—instantly sobered and in his right mind.

Now this was 1970 and different from today—no one did hard drugs or even joked about such in an upper middle-class family.

My father would never admit it, but he knew Bruce drank alcohol in college. Nevertheless, he would've never believed Bruce would do any kind of drugs, let alone LSD—we just didn't do things like that.

Bruce knew that no one in our family would never even joke about such. He knew my father disciplined with his fist and would've beaten him within an inch of his life if he ever found out that he was doing drugs.

Just a different time back then.

When Bruce calmly said that in front of us, I'm sure that both my father and my jaws had fallen to the ground in utter shock and disbelief.

After the shock wore off, I knew I had to ask him how he had such an experience with God so I could have that experience before I died shortly.

Subsequently, the next day, I deluged Bruce with question after question on what had happened and what it meant to ask the Lord into his life.

Bruce had heard the gospel somewhere, previously, but had not responded until on that bad acid trip.

He told me how to repent and ask the Lord into my heart.

I tried.

I didn't feel anything.

Bruce always had major fireworks.

I felt nothing.

I got very discouraged.

THE DEVIL TRIED TO DESTROY ME

For the next six to eight months, I languished, knowing I was dying and without hope.

I wasn't even seeing the cloud puffs any longer.

I was in a very dark place since I believed I had caused my mother's death; and to top things off, later when my father found out about my cancer he hid the information from everyone, including me—even though I already knew, of course. Instead, all he could do was lie and fraudulently take out a MASSIVE insurance policy on me. That made me more depressed. But now I was full of anger. I was full of hate. I was suicidal.

So, not surprisingly, I got swooped up into all the wrong things.

I started drinking and became the second biggest drinker in my high school, only second to my best drinking buddy. I was so proud that I could down a fifth of whiskey in two hours.

How I drove home was a miracle, most likely, many thanks to a lot of (badly bruised) angels who were pushing my car and/or motorcycle back and forth on the road so I didn't wreck and die.

During this time, I bought an old '49 Harley in boxes, fixed it up, built it into a chopper, and started riding with motorcycle gangs.

I was being pulled in the wrong direction by the ruler of this world.

"As for you, you were dead in your transgressions and sins, in which you used to live when you followed the ways of this world and of the ruler of the kingdom of the air (the prince of the power of the air), the spirit who is now at work in those who are disobedient." (Ephesians 2:1–2)

Hard to believe, but the devil didn't have my best interest at heart.

No duh!

I devised a plan to blackmail my father about the insurance fraud, take the money, drive to the Grand Canyon, and drive my chopper off to my death. If I was going to die, I was dying on my own terms!

Also, because of the anger and hate that now consumed me for my father, I also planned to write a letter detailing all the events, fraud, including timelines. Then attach it to my body so that when they picked up the pieces at the bottom, he would be found out, at minimum lose the total payout, as well as the additional he had to pay me in the blackmail, and then, hopefully go to jail.

Payback's a bitch!

Unfortunately, my chopper was so unreliable that it would blow head gaskets all the time. I was tearing it down and rebuilding it each and every week. I could never get it running good enough to leave town. Gee, I wonder who kept messing up my plans?

Then one day, toward the end of that six to eight months, I was out one night, carousing with my biker gang buddies. We were sitting on our parked bikes, drinking bottle after bottle of cheap wine.

I don't know why or what started it, but we got into a spiritual discussion. I told them about what happened to Bruce and that nothing had happened to me. They seemed very interested. They didn't condemn or ridicule him or me.

In that moment, as I said nothing had happened to me, a light came on—ALL OF A SUDDEN, IN AN INSTANT—I realized that that was *NOT* true.

In that moment, I realized that I had the *Greatest Peace* in my heart which could *NOT* be explained.

All of a sudden, I, too, was instantly sobered—as had happened to Bruce.

I told my "friends" I had to leave.

A NEW BEGINNING

The next day, I decided to quit drinking and did so with NO withdrawals—as well as the whole Grand Cannon plan was off.

Immediately, I starting telling everyone about the Love of the Father.

I no longer cared that I was dying—that was a "given"—but now I knew, without question, where I was going. I was filled with joy. I was at peace with it all.

As I stated, this was early in the Charismatic movement where we saw many miracles. I was one; I just didn't know it.

Long story short, not to bore you to death, God led me from one Christian meeting to another until I found the church He wanted me to be a part.

There I thrived. I learned. I grew spiritually.

I knew the Power of God and that He could heal anyone—if, and when, He wanted. I saw it day after day, but I was totally *OKAY* that He didn't heal me and I'd be "going home" to be with Him soon.

VOICE OF GOD

Let's take a short tangent here to interject about hearing the voice of God.

The audible voice of God just doesn't happen too much that I know of. God did it numerous times in the Bible and, in an extreme case, with me.

Most of the time, though, we hear God in a still small voice within.

First Kings 19:11–12 tells us,

"And behold, the Lord passed by, and a great and strong wind rent the mountains and broke in pieces the rocks before the Lord.

But the LORD was NOT in the WIND;

And after the wind, an earthquake,

But the LORD was NOT in the EARTHQUAKE;

And after the earthquake, a fire,

But the LORD was NOT in the FIRE;

And after the fire

[A Sound of Gentle Stillness] A STILL, SMALL VOICE."

God's voice is typically not in the audible.

Nor in the wind, nor in the earthquake, nor in the fire.

It's the still small voice.

But we need to learn to listen.

Carefully.

Correctly.

In Psalm 46:10, we're told,

"Be still, and know that I AM God."

Philippians 4:7 says,

"And the Peace of God, which surpasses ALL understanding (comprehension), will guard your hearts and your minds in Christ Jesus."

So, how do we know it's Him?

We know it's Him because of His Peace that passes understanding. We'll talk more about that later.

RIDING HOME

I was constantly studying the Word and talking to Him about it.

I had dedicated my remaining life and time to Him and with it being the tangible movement of God at the time, I was hearing His still small voice a lot. Which, by the way, any of us can have that same relationship with the Father anytime.

One night, I was riding on my motorcycle, heading home from a meeting. We all joked that we had meetings six days a week and twice on Sunday, but that was really pretty much the truth.

As I was riding along, God spoke to me and said, "Do you see in Isaiah where I said healing was going to happen (in the future) with Jesus?"

"But He was wounded for our transgressions, He was bruised for our guilt and iniquities; the chastisement [needful to obtain] peace and well-being for us was upon Him, and with the stripes [that wounded] Him we are healed and made whole." (Isaiah 53:5)

I answered, "Yes."

"Do you see in First Peter where I said the healing happened (in the past)?"

"He himself bore our sins in His body on the cross, so that we might die to sins and live for righteousness; by His wounds you have been healed." (1 Peter 2:24)

I answered, "Yes."

He said, "Isaiah was looking forward to the cross, and Peter was looking back to the cross. *ALL* was completed at the cross."

Then He said, "Do you want to receive that healing?"

I innocently, nonchalantly said, "Sure"—and in that instant I felt the change and knew I was!

And the rock-hard tumor that had grown for a year and a half in my abdomen from the size of a walnut to larger than a football—just dissipated, melted, completely vanished within 24 hours—at which time my abdomen returned to normal.

CHAPTER TWO

YOU MAY NOT AGREE WITH ME AND I DON'T CARE

ROUGH AROUND THE EDGES

I'M A BIT ROUGH around the edges—some might say, "A lot."

When I first met the Lord, I was a religious, spiritual weirdo. I had good intentions. I meant well, yet I still took the grand prize for many years.

Somehow I thought that if I was the most dedicated believer, I'd deserve to get closer to the Lord. He'd saved me. He'd healed me. He'd shown me the true love I had been missing all my life, so I thought that was the least I could do.

The problem is we cannot do anything to be worthy or good enough to reach God or stay in His Presence.

First, it's by His Grace *alone*.

Ephesians 2:8–9 says,

"For by grace you have been saved through faith; and that not of yourselves, it is the gift of God; not as a result of (any) works, so that no one may boast."

Second, our righteousness, on our very best day, is like filthy rags.

"For we have all become like one who is unclean [ceremonially, like a leper], and all our righteousness (our best deeds of rightness and justice) are like filthy rags or a polluted garment." (Isaiah 64:6)

And, third, at our very best, we're unworthy servants.

"Even so on your part, when you have done everything that was assigned and commanded you, say, we are unworthy servants [possessing no merit, for we have not gone beyond our obligation]; we have [merely] done what was our duty to do." (Luke 17:10)

God loved me anyway, and I loved Him.

FINALLY, GOD BROKE ME OF MY FAKE RELIGIOSITY

Because He loves us, He allows us to go through trials and tribulations—sometimes horrendous trials and tribulations—which is for our good.

"God has said, 'Never will I leave you; never will I forsake you.'" (Hebrews 13:5)

"And we know that God causes all things to work together for good to those who love God, to those who are called according to His purpose." (Romans 8:28)

"We boast in the hope of the glory of God. Not only so, but we also glory in our sufferings, because we know that suffering produces perseverance; perseverance, character; and character, hope. And hope does not put us to shame, because God's Love has been poured out into our hearts through the Holy Spirit, who has been given to us." (Romans 5:2–5)

Hence, He "graciously" put me through (or allowed me to go through) HELL in numerous areas—my wife, my job, my kids, my church, my health, and more. Everything was falling apart.

So, with all sarcasm intended, "Thanks Papa."

It all came to a head when I was at my wits' end in the upper eighties.

WAITING FOR LIGHTNING TO STRIKE

I used to work eighty- to one-hundred-hour weeks. I was leaving work at my normal 2:00 a.m. time, heading out into a mostly empty parking lot.

I was talking to the Lord per normal, BUT THIS TIME, I'D HAD IT.

I WAS PISSED!

So I stopped in the middle of the parking lot and started yelling at the top of my lungs, cussing out the Lord.

Yeah, the same One whom I claimed I loved.

For the next ten to twenty minutes—nonstop.

I ranted! I raved! I yelled! I screamed!

At the top of my lungs, I cussed Him out with the most hideous words I could think of in that moment.

I used words I thought I'd forgot.

I spewed out words I didn't know I knew.

I told Him to go to hell.

I was sure this was the end.

I was expecting lightning to strike, and I knew I deserved it!

I didn't care.

I paused.

I was waiting for Him to yell back at me before He struck me dead.

Finally, very calmly, He said, "Are you done yet?"

Him saying it calmly just pissed me off more, so I yelled more—a lot more.

Finally. I was totally exhausted. I couldn't have yelled another word if I tried. I stopped to receive the punishment I knew was due.

Again, He very calmly said, "Are you done now?"

Ashamed, I said, "Yes."

Now I was just awaiting my punishment, but it did not come.

Instead, I just felt His BOUNDLESS LOVE surrounding me.

"Why?" I asked. "Why don't you punish me like I deserve?"

He said, "Because I love you."

I said, "But I just cussed you out. I told you to go to hell. I spewed the worse things to You than I've ever said to anyone before. Aren't I the worst person ever? Especially, since I'm supposed to be a believer and a good Christian?"

He said, "No. You didn't surprise me. I already knew what was in your heart. I just wanted you to find out what was in there."

YOU SEE, GOD IS THE GOD OF TRUTH

In Isaiah 65:16, we're told,

"Whoever invokes a blessing in the land will do so by the God of Truth; Whoever takes an oath in the land will swear by the God of Truth."

And in John 8:31–32,

"So Jesus said, 'if you continue in My word, then you are truly disciples of Mine; and you will know the Truth, and the Truth will make you free.'"

"Jesus said, 'I AM the Way and the Truth and the Life; no one comes to the Father except by [through] Me.'" (John 14:6)

The real you doesn't scare Him. He'd rather have the true you, with all your faults, versus a fake one, so be your true self at all times.

You can never be good enough for the Lord, so stop trying.

After learning that lesson, now I'm just an honest "you get what you see" person. If you don't like it, sorry! I really don't care. I'm not living for your approval. I'm not religious anymore.

I know that the real me—the good, the bad, and yes, the ugly—is just fine with Papa God.

So if you find out that I'm not perfect—and I let some of my roughness out in this manual—get over it! He will.

A WORD TO THE WISE

Don't be religious. Don't try to fake out yourself, others, or God.

Be real. Be honest. Love the Truth.

We can never be perfect enough.

We can never be good enough.

Note: Sometimes I will repeat myself in this manual. Hopefully, that means it was important and worth repeating.

It's by grace we've been saved, not on our own or anything by our righteousness—at best, we are unworthy servants.

All we can do is use the ONLY power we've been given, which is choice and yielding.

Since you can never be good enough on your own—stop trying—start yielding.

Here's a secret you will learn in this manual (that I will repeat over and over and over). "We're a vessel to whomever we yield."

THE CHURCH

FORSAKE NOT THE ASSEMBLY OF THE BRETHREN

Hebrews 10:25 says,

"Not forsaking the assembly of believers."

Forsaking in the Greek is 'egkataleipō' (en-kat-a-lee-po), meaning to "leave behind," "desert," "abandon," "forsake."

In case you're not spotting it, the wording "Not forsaking" is very NEGATIVE. God didn't say, "Have a good old time hanging out with the brethren." He said, "Don't forsake them."

Have you ever wondered why God said it in such a NEGATIVE way? Because sometimes—maybe many times—the assembly is worthy of forsaking or abandoning.

I don't hate God's people when we talk about the Church being the assembly of the saints or the brethren. I just hate religions, religiosity, religious institutions, services, denominations, and buildings—all called "the church." Most stink.

Remember, this is coming from someone who went to meetings six days a week and twice on Sunday.

So, why the disdain from God's point of view? And, mine? Because, men (and women) get in the way of God and His will. Most of these people call themselves "leaders," creating religiosity, creating institutions, creating denominations.

I'm going to go off on one of my tangents here for a moment—one of the many that you will get with me—it's just part of who I am—so get over it.

Let's look at the name "denomination" and do a little play on words.

"Denom" is "demon" if you reverse two letters—then you can find in order, the words "in," then "a," and back up two letters and find "nation." Therefore, "denomination" is "demon-in-a-nation."

Have you ever thought of it that way before—that "denominations" are "demons in nations"—that have demon rulers ruling over, controlling, separating, dividing believers into segregated, separated, isolated, unwilling to change, unwilling to bend, unwilling to come together religious groups?

You might think that's unfair of me to say such a thing—since you know your religion and your denomination is good—you know "we're not that way." Well, no one ever said I was going to be fair, or nice, or coddle to your delicate needs, and not offend. In case you haven't noticed by now, I'm not afraid to offend—if I believe what I'm telling you is true.

"Better is open rebuke than love that is concealed. Faithful are the wounds of a friend, but deceitful are the kisses of an enemy." (Proverbs 27:5-6)

So if you let that sink in—that denominations are demons in nations—then you might begin to perceive that the ruler of this world is behind ALL OF THE DIVISIONS in the Church. If you don't fully grasp that importance now, you'll understand why this is so important later.

Let's get back to the main subject at hand. It can be anyone, but it's usually not the people, saints, brethren, sheep that cause the worst stink. It's the leaders, who have been given responsibility over the sheep. They're the ones that the majority of the time really screw things up.

Keep in mind most of the time God's people are just responding to or following the leaders.

I also mentioned services and buildings. I've seen too many gatherings that love their services and buildings more than the Lord Himself and His Anointing.

I hate when men and women try to "run" or "control" God's Anointing, His Presence, the Word incarnate in the gathering of the Body, the Saints, the real Church.

WESTERN FALLACY

Leaders think they're at the top of the food chain. They want to be in charge, but Galatians 5:26 says,

"Let us not become boastful and self-conceited, competitive and challenging and provoking and irritating to one another, envying and being jealous of one another."

We will talk more about this later, but just note for now, we must end the pervasive Western view of leadership in the Church.

We need to come to a place in our hearts, our minds, and our actions to let God do His thing or do NOTHING.

But you say, "When we do that, there will be a lot of crap along the way," and you would definitely be right. With babies come a lot of poop. So what?

Because along with the Good—NO, the GREAT—will come the release of the Anointing, the Presence, and the Power of God!

It'll be during the crappy times when men and women will want to take over, but this is the time to just say, "NO."

Our puny minds can't perceive. This might just be God's plan, a test from the Father to see if we can permit Him the opportunity to show us what He can do, or will we intervene like always, which is our predictable human nature?

Even though at times it will stink more than the worse poopy diaper, or a better example is an animal rendering plant (which is the worse!), don't forsake the assembly—God's people, the Church. Don't throw out the baby with the bath water.

In Acts and the beginning of the Charismatic movement, we had a lot of meetings, house-to-house. Yes, we did have meetings in larger church buildings, but that's where a greater percentage of egos and personalities surfaced, wanting to overlord and take control. Unfortunately, it just messed things up.

Big meetings can be "okay" if God is truly in charge. Otherwise, I'm not for them. See how I said that in such a NEGATIVE way? If the Father can do it, so can I.

I humor myself.

We need to declare to those who think they are the ministers, pastors, teachers, evangelists, prophets, and apostles that they CANNOT be in control or have the power. If so, that would eliminate a lot of the crap.

Read more on how to find that balance later.

TITHES IS ANOTHER BIG FALLACY

I know that most churches—and especially their leaders—will disagree and hate me for this, but I really don't give a rat's a$$.

I know churches waste a lot of time preaching and teaching on tithing, twisting the ol' ten percent to the order of Melchizedek in Hebrews 7:1–28, which is BS. All who do so do not know what they're talking about or are just charlatans.

While the tithe was true for the priests of Levi in the Old Testament—they were never part of the order of Melchizedek. Neither the Levitical priesthood or the order of Melchizedek carries over to the leaders in the New Testament—as today's leaders promote and would like us to believe. All ended with Jesus.

The Law of Moses was the law of sin and death, true in the Old Testament. This was replaced by the death, resurrection, and the Blood of Jesus. That gave us the law of Life, which set us free from the law of sin and death.

The same verses, along with the conclusion in Hebrews 8:1, states that Jesus is the fulfillment of that Melchizedek priesthood. Therefore, the TITHE goes to HIM—NOT the churches, ministers, leaders, or any type of ministries.

Note: It was only recorded one time in the New Testament where the saints were told to gather tithes or contributions.

It was NOT for the local church.

It was NOT for supporting the local leaders to pay their livelihood.

It was NOT to build new buildings.

It was NOT even to help start or support ministries.

It was to help the brethren in another city as they were in great need in a time of famine.

"Through the Spirit predicted that a severe famine would spread over the entire Roman world... And, in the proportion that the disciples, as each one was able, determined to send a contribution for the relief of the brethren living in Judea, and this they did." (Acts 11:28–30)

Therefore, let those who minister, pastor, teach, etc., do so for FREE—not for want of money.

In my personal opinion, do NOT pay them a salary.

Let them work regular jobs, and do this in parallel, out of conviction and in relationship to the Lord.

Wow, I am such a blasphemous person now, right?

I'm going to go on another tangent here—I warned you, but you wouldn't listen—too late now, you're stuck.

This is exactly the same—how leaders in every level of government should operate—in the church and in secular governing as our (Christian) founding fathers intended. No lifetime positions. No (or very little) salaries. No long-term or lifetime benefits.

That'd eliminate a lot of charlatans and wolves in sheep's clothing right there alone. At least it would take the issue of money off the table. Of course, there are other concerns, which we will talk about later.

I believe after putting the Lord first, we should take care of our responsibilities, our families, ourselves, our businesses or jobs, our community (church and secular), our country, and voting.

Yes, Christians should vote.

But I digress.

We live in this world, but that doesn't mean we're of this world. We MUST do ALL we need to do here yet never forget whose we are.

We need to find the balance, recognizing that only the Lord can teach us that balance.

We should keep our eyes and hearts toward Heaven but keep our minds and feet on the earth. Thereby, we will be able to fulfill the duties we've been given in both.

It should be obvious. Don't worship the duties nor anything else. Worship the Lord.

So forget about tithes. Matter of fact, quit collecting them.

If that means we can't have big church buildings and lands, so what!

Oh no! You mean no more megachurches?

Could be.

Now that you're probably confused and/or pissed at me, do remember we are to give a tithe—just not necessarily to churches or ministers.

What did Hebrews say? We are to give our tithes to Jesus, the Melchizedek High Priest.

What does that mean?

Gee whiz. It means that we might just actually need to take the time to pray and hear from God and find out what we're supposed to do each month with our tithes.

Maybe things like feed the poor, help the needy, take care of the sick, the orphans, and the widows, maybe give to angels unaware—who knows?

Can we sometimes give a part of our tithes to churches? Ministries? Or, ministers?

Yes, if that's what the Father is *saying* to do.

23

Here's the answer.

Pray first. Pray every time. *Wait until you've heard, then do it.*

No rote.

Sounds like work. Yup! But it's worth it.

Once we get past the poopy bathwater, with the real baby remaining, it is a very important place for growth—for teaching, for pastoring, for overseeing the flock (the saints), for loving, for caring for the body and others, as well as feeding the poor, widows, and orphans.

WHY THE CHARISMATIC MOVEMENT DIED

I was told that the Charismatic movement started in 1968, but as I said, I wasn't birthed until 1970, so all I know is from that point forward.

WHAT GOT IN THE WAY?

Unfortunately, in my observations, of the limited number of years the movement lasted, men and women, pride, ego, seeking power and control of the movement all got in the way.

Leaders became overlords, not overseers.

The fallacy and nature of men (and women) is that they want to be overlords, but the plan of God is they are to be overseers.

THE DAY IT DIED

Somewhere around 1977 was when "they," the "designated men in charge" (sorry, ladies) decided that the movement had "evolved" into two denominations—the "faith movement" and the "discipleship movement"—with no other options.

We were told we had to choose between the two.

Both the basic teachings of faith and discipleship were true in themselves, yet both were rubbish that they should or ever could control God's movement.

It was garbage that God's divine intervention with men and women could ever be regulated by men and women, but unfortunately, that's what we do. We can always f— up a good thing.

Sorry if you can't handle my crudeness. This is the last time I'll apologize for such. If you want to throw out the baby with the bath water, you have free will. Exercise it. Stop here, and put down the manual, or get over it and continue. Your choice.

So the Spirit of God left our presence and our meetings, and we got the result of our endeavors, which were simply gatherings, churches, denominations without the overflowing Presence of the Lord.

Sure, there might be some tiny remnants of His Presence in some of the churches today, but nothing like what it was before.

I will correct myself here because I believe we're on the verge of the next real release of the Power of God and His next upcoming movement.

Examples are the recent mini-movements that happened at Asbury College and Texas A&M in early 2023.

I'd bet that those going through these two movements wouldn't call them mini, but compared to what He's done in the past and will do in the future, they are.

These are a merely a very small taste of what is to come.

But will we destroy His movement—again?

Will men and women try to control God—again?

Are we that stupid?

Unfortunately, YES, YES, and YES.

I'd love to be proven wrong.

See my warnings throughout this manual.

DICK

I'm going to stop here for a moment and interject that I'd needed a good spiritual father figure in my life. From 1970 on, Dick, became that person for me.

Dick was one of the local leaders in our church, but in 1977, he also was perplexed over the decisions being forced upon us to move into one of the two "new denominations"—seemingly to be the only options.

Dick asked me, "I know you believe in both faith and discipleship. I also know that you don't prescribe to either movement. So, what will you do? Which one will you join?"

I replied, "Neither. And as of this day, I never want to be called a Charismatic again." Perplexed, Dick asked, "Then what are you?"

I answered, "From now on, I only want to be known as a Christian."

SPIRITUAL WARFARE

What does this all of this have to do with spiritual warfare?

Everything.

How can we fight a spiritual enemy who is far more powerful than us if we don't have our relationship right with the ONLY One who can?

Bottom line—you might agree with me in whole, in part, or not at all; but if you can, look beyond any offense you may think I've caused and continue reading this manual then decide for yourselves as you listen before the Lord to determine what's the baby and what's the bathwater.

Be sure to save the baby!

CHAPTER THREE

HOW I GOT INTO SPIRITUAL WARFARE

MY EXPERIENCES

I SAW A LOT.

I experienced a lot.

I learned a lot.

I don't claim to know it all, but what I have, I will share.

ENEMY LAUGHING AT ME

As a new believer, I was studying and praying in my family room at home alone except for my dog, Jezreel.

Yup, the same family room, where I used to see visions of time, was now my prayer and study room.

As I sat in my easy chair, praying, I got distracted. I heard an extremely tiny but very weird laughing voice just outside my ear, not from some far distance away.

Instead of ignoring this distraction, as I should've, I chose to listen more. I strained to hear it better.

Somehow, I knew I shouldn't be doing it, but I wanted to know what was that weird (wicked sounding) laughing voice.

In making that decision, I gave an opening, yielding to that evil spirit to begin to oppress me. In just a matter of seconds, the tiny audible voice got louder and louder and LOUDER until it was literally a booming voice, filling the room with wicked laughter.

It surrounded me with terror. For some long moments, I could not move. I could not speak. It paralyzed me with fear.

Finally, I was able to barely call out and said the name *Jesus*. I began calling out on Him more. The more I did, the more the paralysis, the fear, and the voice slowly subsided—until I could finally YELL, "In the name of Jesus!" and the spirits were quieted.

Still shaken, I stood up, wobbly, and walked over to the sliding door, opened it, and started yelling, demanding that the spirits leave. I kept repeating, "Go!" "Leave in the name of Jesus!" and "Don't come back!"

I stood there, pointing and waving my arm, sending the unseen demons out the door. I was very young in the Lord and we all were very dramatic back then.

Poor Jez. He thought I was scolding him. Head down, he slowly sulked, heading out the door. He looked back at me with sad bewildering eyes, wondering what he'd done wrong. I grabbed him by collar and said, "Not you, Jez!" and slammed the door shut.

Lessons learned.

I should've NEVER listened.

NEVER entertained the temptation.

NEVER yielded to those spirits.

I had opened myself up to both a spirit of fear and a paralyzing spirit.

Just dumb.

DOING BATTLE WITH STEP-MOTHER FOR SIX MONTHS

Several years after my mother passed, Marge married my father and moved in.

I was nineteen, still living at home, and going to college.

During the day, Marge and I were cordial to one another, but at night and night after night, for six months, I would be doing battle with her in the spirit.

Then one evening, she and my father were sitting at the dining room table, quietly reading the paper, spending time together per their normal routine.

Sidenote: My father wasn't a believer yet. Actually, YES and NO—but more about that in the next book. At this point in life he was a "nothing" by his own words.

Feeling it was finally the right time, I sat down at the table, looked Marge straight in the eyes, and out of the blue said, "So, you're a witch, aren't you?"

My father was like! "What the hell?"

Immediately she replied, "Yes, I am."

She went on to say, "I've been a witch all my life, and I come from a long line of witches."

I said, "I knew you were."

I went on. "Matter of fact, you and I have been doing battle in the spirit night after night for the last six months."

Aghast that I was offending his new bride, my father exclaimed again! "What in the hell are you talking about?"

Before I could answer, she laughed and happily responded, "YES! Night after night, I continue to cast spells against you, but I can feel you doing battle against them, and they just don't work."

This was another time my father's jaw hit the ground.

A couple of years later, Marge and my father starting going to a Methodist church that preached the gospel, and they both ended up meeting the Lord.

At that time, she said she quit being a witch.

While a good church, it was not a Spirit-filled church that understood deliverance, so, unfortunately, that didn't happen.

Eventually things seemed to reverse—as is typical if the doors aren't closed and the room isn't filled correctly.

We will discuss these things in more detail later.

BEST BOOKS EVER TO GAIN INSIGHT INTO THE SPIRITUAL REALM

Even though fiction, I love the books by Frank E. Peretti.

This Present Darkness and *Piercing the Darkness*—they give a great view of the spiritual realms and battles we can't perceive by natural senses. They show what goes on beyond what our eyes can see or our ears can hear.

If you've never read them, I highly recommend them.

CHAPTER FOUR

IN CHRIST

THIS MAY BE NEWS TO SOME, BUT CHRIST IS NOT JESUS'S LAST NAME

THE WORD *CHRIST* ACTUALLY means "the ANOINTING."

In turn, "the ANOINTING" comes by "the HOLY SPIRIT" flowing through us.

Let's look at a few scriptures to see how *CHRIST* is equated to the ANOINTING and the HOLY SPIRIT and how easily they can be interchanged.

"You know of Jesus of Nazareth, how God ANOINTED Him with the HOLY SPIRIT and with Power, and how He went about doing good and healing all." (Acts 10:38)

"Therefore, there is now no condemnation for those who are In CHRIST Jesus, because through CHRIST Jesus, the law of the [HOLY] SPIRIT who gives life, has set you free." (Romans 8:1–2)

"I am telling the truth in CHRIST, I am not lying, my conscience testifies with me in the HOLY SPIRIT." (Romans 9:1)

"For no matter how many promises God has made, they are 'Yes' In CHRIST... Now it is God who makes both us and you Stand firm In CHRIST. He ANOINTED us, set His seal of ownership on us, and put His [HOLY] SPIRIT in our hearts as a deposit, guaranteeing what is to come." (2 Corinthians 1:20–22)

Christ is the Greek word 'Christos' (cray-stos), which means "the Anointed One." It is from the primary root word 'chriō' (cree-oo), which means "to anoint" or "anointed."

In the Hebrew, the root words for anointing are 'mashach' (mee-shack), which means "anoint," "anointed," "anointing," "oil," and 'yitshar' (yeets-hawr), which means "fresh oil," "oil," "anointed," "anointing."

Also, note here that OIL is the biblical symbol for the HOLY SPIRIT, so to be "In CHRIST" means to be "in the ANOINTING," the FRESH OIL ("the HOLY SPIRIT") from God.

I'm biased. I love the Anointing of the Holy Spirit flowing through us.

As yielded believers, we all should.

In the early days, when God's Presence was so thick you could cut it with a knife, we could wait before Him for hours. There was nothing better—waiting before Him, not moving until He decided to move. Simply stated, His Presence was worth it!

Maybe the Quakers of old were on to something.

We, the Church, typically make the mistake, feeling like "we must do something," so we do.

We convince ourselves that "something is better than nothing."

Not so.

Instead,

"This is the word of the LORD... 'Not by might, nor by power, but by My [HOLY] SPIRIT [the ANOINTING],' says the LORD of hosts." (Zechariah 4:6)

Yet we continue to "play church," assuming that God will eventually show up.

Again, not so much.

EITHER WAIT FOR THE ANOINTING OR GO HOME

Actually, if you're not coming for the ANOINTING, then just don't come in the first place.

I know that many well-meaning people and leaders would argue with me about this statement, saying we've been busy doing things for God and His Presence does show up.

Therefore, I must be wrong—VERY WRONG!

Actually, I will correct myself here. God does love and honor His people operating out of ignorance and limited understanding, yet caring, trying so hard, expending so much effort to create an environment for Him.

Remember the altars the people of Israel would build each time God showed up in a big way. It was a tribute to that wonderful moment in time. They built them so they could come back and find God there again.

Sadly, did you notice that God's Presence (SPIRIT) never showed up at any of those altars ever again?

NEVER.

They just became an empty pile of stones.

We do the same.

Consequently, nowadays, as a reward of well-meaning people's efforts wanting and seeking Him, unaware of how to really reach Him, God does give them a tiny taste—dribbles—of what they could have.

Maybe they get one hundredth of 1 percent of His Presence.

Maybe one tenth of 1 percent.

Maybe 1 percent on their very best day—if they're lucky.

Unfortunately, like Israel, they'll build "spiritual altars" to that last big moment, action, or function, thinking if they do it again, repeating the same exact things done the same exact way, they'll find God's Presence there for a second, third, and forth time.

But they won't.

Accepting the tiny limited Presence as if no one else can do better as they make comparisons to other churches to justify themselves. They end up making the mistake, thinking they've arrived, but they haven't.

It's true that even the crumbs from the table are better than nothing, but is that what you're willing to settle for?

Why would you give up for so little?

But what if you could have 5 percent?

How about 10 percent?

How about 20 percent?

How about more?

What would that look like?

If they only knew better.

Once again, I digress.

BACK TO CHRIST

For giggles, let's look to see how many scriptures change, become alive, and have greater clarity when you replace "CHRIST" or the "HOLY SPIRIT" with "the ANOINTING."

"To present to you the Word of God in its FULLNESS—the MYSTERY that has been KEPT HIDDEN for ages... the glorious riches of this MYSTERY, which is CHRIST [the ANOINTING] in you, the HOPE of GLORY." (Colossians 1:25–27)

"In order that they may KNOW the MYSTERY of GOD, namely, CHRIST [the ANOINTING], in whom are hidden all the TREASURES of WISDOM and KNOWLEDGE. (Colossians 2:2–3)

"GRACE and TRUTH came through Jesus CHRIST [the ANOINTING]." (John 1:17)

"When you were dead in your sins and in the uncircumcision of your flesh, GOD MADE YOU ALIVE with CHRIST [the ANOINTING]." (Colossians 2:13)

"The REALITY [substance], however, is found in CHRIST [the ANOINTING]... Since you died with CHRIST [the ANOINTING] to the elemental spiritual forces of this world." (Colossians 2:16–17, 20)

"Since, then, YOU HAVE BEEN RAISED with [in] CHRIST [the ANOINTING], set your hearts on things above, where CHRIST [the ANOINTING] is, seated at the RIGHT HAND OF GOD. Set your minds on things above, not on earthly things. For you died, and YOUR LIFE is NOW HIDDEN with CHRIST [the ANOINTING] in God. When CHRIST [the ANOINTING], who is your life, appears, then you also WILL APPEAR WITH HIM in GLORY. (Colossians 3:1–4)

"So, in CHRIST [the ANOINTING] Jesus, you are ALL CHILDREN of GOD through faith.

For all of you who were BAPTIZED into CHRIST [the ANOINTING] have CLOTHED YOURSELVES with CHRIST [the ANOINTING].

There is neither JEW nor GENTILE, neither SLAVE nor FREE, nor is there MALE and FEMALE, for YOU are ALL ONE, in CHRIST [the ANOINTING]." (Galatians 3:26–28)

And, while there are many more, finally,

"Therefore, if anyone be In CHRIST [the ANOINTING], he is a new creature; old things are passed away; behold, all things are becoming new." (2 Corinthians 5:17)

Sidenote: Before any ladies get their panties in a wad about the Bible always saying "he this" or "he that" and feeling slighted such as "he is a new creature" above, please remember the scripture just previous. It states when we are in CHRIST (the ANOINTING), there is neither MALE or FEMALE. So if we abide in CHRIST, doesn't that change a bunch of things for ALL of us throughout the scriptures?

That would be a "no duh."

THE FULLNESS OF GOD

Continuing on in slightly different direction.

"That He would grant you, according to the riches of His Glory, to be STRENGTHENED WITH POWER through His SPIRIT [the ANOINTING] in the inner man, so that CHRIST [the ANOINTING] may dwell in your hearts through faith; and, to know the LOVE of CHRIST [the ANOINTING] which SURPASSES KNOWLEDGE, that you may be FILLED UP to the MEASURE of ALL the FULLNESS of GOD." (Ephesians 3:16–19)

"For in CHRIST [the ANOINTING] ALL the FULLNESS of the DEITY (Godhead) lives in bodily form, and in CHRIST [the ANOINTING] you have been brought to FULLNESS." (Colossians 2:9–10)

Recognizing the FULLNESS of God lives in the HOLY SPIRIT, and the HOLY SPIRIT, the ANOINTING, lives in us. Therefore, if we have eyes to see, the FULLNESS of GOD LIVES IN US—and that's true ALL the time—*whether you feel it or not*—not just good days—not when you feel "spiritual" as if then you deserve it—but even on your worst or most sinful day—even the day you cuss out the Lord!

FROM OUR SPIRIT, THROUGH OUR SOUL, AND BODY

"Jesus stood and cried out, saying, 'He who believes in Me, as the Scripture said, from his innermost being will flow RIVERS of LIVING WATER.' But this He spoke of the SPIRIT [the ANOINTING], whom those who believed in Him were to receive." (John 7:37–39)

And,

"In Him, you also, after listening to the message of TRUTH, the gospel of your salvation—having also believed, you WERE SEALED in HIM with the HOLY SPIRIT [the ANOINTING] of promise." (Ephesians 1:13)

Revisiting Second Corinthians 1:20–22 again from this perspective:

"He ANOINTED us, set His SEAL of OWNERSHIP on US, and put His SPIRIT [the ANOINTING] in OUR HEARTS as a DEPOSIT, GUARANTEEING what is to come."

On the day of our salvation, WE WERE SEALED with the promised HOLY SPIRIT (the ANOINTING).

Now, the HOLY SPIRIT (the ANOINTING) RESIDES in OUR SPIRIT, and if we yield, He will flow through our soul, and if we yield more through our body, and beyond.

These are the rivers of living water (the ANOINTING) that will come out of our innermost being when we yield and get out of the way.

ALWAYS REMEMBER

"WE'RE A VESSEL TO WHOMEVER WE YIELD."

Now, hopefully, you can see that, most importantly, we can be a vessel to the Anointing flowing through us.

You may or may not understand this completely—that's alright—but this is not the time to go into the full teaching and understanding about body, soul, and spirit. This we will leave for another time.

Either way, remember to yield.

WARNING: DO NOT WORSHIP THE ANOINTING

While this should be obvious, for some—or many—it's not.

Never be deceived and succumb to the blunder of worshipping the Anointing. If you do, you're falling under another intended misdirection from the enemy, trying to get you to miss, leave behind, one of the greatest things you can ever experience from the Holy Spirit.

Remember, the enemy wants you to miss finding, then centering on the Lord. He doesn't care if you fall to direct sins or if you turn the Glory of God into religiosity, watching the pendulum swing from one extreme to the other, wanting it so bad that you end up missing the Lord Himself.

SIMPLE ANSWER

Only worship the Lord, and the Anointing will be a wonderful byproduct.

CHAPTER FIVE

THE DEVIL IS FIFTY FEET TALL

WHO IS THE ENEMY?

HE'S BEEN CALLED BY MANY NAMES

S ATAN

The Devil

Lucifer

Beelzebub

The Fallen Angel

The Morning Star

Guardian Cherub

Prince (Ruler) of Demons

The Ruler of this World

The Ruler of the Kingdom of the Air

The Prince of the Power of the Air

The Father of Lies

The Tempter

The Great Dragon

And, The Enemy

The enemy is a broad term I will use to describe both the devil and his fallen angels (demons, spirits) throughout this manual.

Satan was God's most powerful cherub, archangel and creation who thought he was greater than God, his creator, and could challenge God, so God cast him to the earth.

"How you have fallen from Heaven, morning star, son of the dawn! You have been cast down to the earth, you who once laid low the nations!

You said in your heart, 'I will ascend to the heavens; I will raise my throne above the stars of God; I will sit enthroned on the mount of assembly, on the utmost heights of Mount Zaphon.

I will ascend above the tops of the clouds; I will make myself like the Most High.'

But you are brought down to the realm of the dead, to the depths of the pit." (Isaiah 14:12–15)

"You were in Eden, the garden of God; every precious stone adorned you...your settings and mountings were made of gold; on the day you were created they were prepared.

You were anointed as a guardian cherub, for so I ordained you.

You were on the holy mount of God; you walked among the fiery stones.

You were blameless in your ways from the day you were created.

Until wickedness was found in you.

Through your widespread trade you were filled with violence, and you sinned.

So, I drove you in disgrace from the mount of God, and I expelled you, guardian cherub, from among the fiery stones.

Your heart became proud on account of your beauty, and you corrupted your wisdom because of your splendor.

So, I threw you to the earth; I made a spectacle of you before kings." (Ezekiel 28:13–17)

Even though cast to earth, he's still God's most powerful cherub, archangel, spirit, and creation.

No longer powerful in Heaven, he's now the most powerful being on and ruling earth.

Never be fooled.

Compared to us, the devil is overwhelmingly powerful, and he can crush us like tiny bugs under his feet.

FIFTY FEET TALL

Let's make some comparisons.

Goliath was a monstrous fighter for the Philistines taunting Israel. It's been estimated that he was somewhere between nine to ten feet tall, probably one of the tallest, largest men ever known to have lived.

His height and size alone scared the whole army of Israel. No one would fight him. He was a monster compared to the five- to six-foot-tall David and other Israelites.

Today, most of us are five to six feet tall—some taller, some shorter.

So when we see some seven-foot-plus basketball players, we think they're giants—yet they're nothing compared to Goliath.

Now there's no known record of how tall and big the devil is, but we're told he was the largest, once greatest (until he fell from grace), most beautiful, and most powerful being that God ever created.

Nowhere in the bible are his dimensions defined. Maybe he's twenty-feet tall. Maybe he's fifty-feet tall. Maybe he's one-hundred-feet tall.

Since we know he's the largest of all God's creations, then for the sake of our analogy, let's designate him to be fifty-feet tall.

If any of us stood next to a ten-foot-tall Goliath, we'd be puny, but even a ten-foot Goliath would look puny compared to a fifty-foot giant; and if any of us stood next to a fifty-foot-tall devil, we'd look like tiny bugs ready to be crushed under his feet.

BOTTOM LINE

The devil being the largest, smartest, once greatest creation of God, we need to recognize we will NEVER be able to win against him on our own—but even a fifty-foot giant's power is limited and finite.

The good news is God is INFINITE.

His Power is without end.

A PLANE TAKING OFF

Let's look at an analogy—like a plane on the ground ready to take off.

When we get on the plane and look out the window, everything looks normal—like how we compare ourselves to others and everything here on the earth, all the same size.

But as the plane takes off and begins to ascend, things on the ground start to become smaller and smaller. People, cars, and the like all begin to look like bugs. Soon houses look like bugs—kind of how the devil sees us.

As the plane ascends further, even fifty-foot buildings and, eventually, skyscrapers begin to look like bugs until we ascend so high we can no longer see any of them.

This is a simple visual analogy to begin to understand what the devil sees but, even more importantly, what is God's Infinite Power.

God's Infinite Power exceeds far beyond how high the plane could ascend. God's Infinite Power exceeds beyond what any rocket could ascend.

Infinite means NO LIMITS.

Our power is nothing compared to the devil.

The devil's power is nothing compared to God.

ANOTHER GREAT VISUAL

Remember geometry class?

Let's create a baseline and then draw a line from the base up, six feet. Each end has "end points." Therefore, in geometry, it's called a "line"; and, by definition, a line is finite and limited.

This represents us.

Then next to it, let's draw a second line from the base up, fifty feet. Again, each end has "end points." Therefore, again a "line" and again, by definition, is finite and limited.

This represents the devil.

Then next to both, draw a third line again from the base but much taller than both others and with an arrow on top. That type of line is called a

46

"ray." It continues upward FOREVER and, by definition, is INFINITE and UNLIMITED.

This represents God.

We, as the six-foot line, are finite.

Compared to the fifty-foot devil, we're small and could easily be crushed, but he's also finite.

Now let's compare both to God. Here God is an INFINITE ray extending into ETERNITY. All other lines become smaller and smaller and smaller until they're out of sight and are NOTHING in comparison to Him.

Therefore, we are not to depend upon our (finite) power, nor are we to cower under the devil's (finite) power even though much greater than ours. Instead, we are to yield ourselves and depend upon the Infinite God of the universe who has UNLIMITED Power.

A SECRET ~ SITTING AT THE RIGHT HAND OF GOD

In view of finite lines (of us and the devil) compared to the infinite ray of God, let's take a new look at "In Christ" from Colossians 3 from the chapter above where it says,

"Since, then, you have been raised with (in) CHRIST [the ANOINTING], set your hearts on things above, where CHRIST [the ANOINTING] is, SEATED at the RIGHT HAND of GOD. Set your minds on things above, not on earthly things. For you died, and YOUR LIFE is now HIDDEN with CHRIST [the ANOINTING] in God."

Can you catch the *AMAZING PICTURE* God just gave us here?

Let's review from a new perspective.

We're finite with very limited power.

The devil is also finite but with a hell of a lot more power compared to us.

God is Infinite, but neither us nor the devil have any power (zero) compared to Him.

HERE'S THE SECRET

CHRIST is seated at the Right Hand of the Father.

Therefore, when we are In CHRIST, In the ANOINTING, we then rise up from our lowly six-foot finite level to the INFINITE level of God, now seated, In CHRIST, at God's Right Hand.

From this new perspective In CHRIST, we can see from God's viewpoint that the enemy is nothing.

Now before you "feel your oats" and somehow think you're "all that and a bag of chips," *YOU'RE NOT!*

We didn't do a damn thing different, not one thing better.

It's all about staying In CHRIST, In the ANOINTING, and that's not a given.

It's only when you get out of the way and let God.

We will talk about that more—soon.

WHEN ON GOD'S SIDE, WE'RE PROTECTED, HIDDEN UNDER HIS WING

"He who DWELLS in the secret place (shelter) of the Most High will REST, and shall remain stable, and fixed under the shadow of the Almighty

[Whose Power NO foe can withstand].

'He is my Refuge and my Fortress, my God; on Him I lean, and rely, and in Him I [confidently] trust!'

He will DELIVER you from the snare of the fowler, and from the deadly pestilence.

He will COVER you with His feathers, and under His wings shall you TRUST, and find REFUGE;

His TRUTH, and His FAITHFULNESS are a shield and a buckler.

You shall NOT BE AFRAID of the terror of the night,

NOR of the arrow (the evil plots and slanders of the wicked) that flies by day,

NOR of the pestilence that stalks in darkness,

NOR of the destruction, and sudden death that surprise, and lay waste at noonday.

A thousand may fall at your side, and ten thousand at your right hand,

But it shall NOT come near you.

You will only OBSERVE with YOUR EYES [YOURSELF INACCESSIBLE in the SECRET PLACE of the Most High],

As you witness the reward (punishment) of the wicked.

Because you have made the Lord your REFUGE, and the Most High your DWELLING PLACE,

There shall NO harm will overtake you,

NO evil befall you, NOR any plague, or calamity come near your tent.

For He will COMMAND, give His angels [especial] charge over you,

To GUARD you, to ACCOMPANY, and DEFEND, and PRESERVE you in all your ways [of obedience and service].

...YOU SHALL TREAD UPON the lion and adder;

The young lion, and the serpent, YOU WILL TRAMPLE UNDERFOOT.

Because he has SET HIS LOVE upon Me,

Therefore, will I DELIVER (RESCUE) him; I will PROTECT him, and SET him on high,

Because he knows, and acknowledges, and understands My Name.

[has a PERSONAL KNOWLEDGE of My Mercy, Love, and Kindness—TRUSTS and RELIES on Me, knowing I will never forsake him, no, NEVER].

He shall CALL upon Me, and I will ANSWER him;

I will be WITH him in trouble, I will DELIVER him and HONOR him.

With long life will I SATISFY him, and show him My SALVATION." (Psalm 91:1–16)

SO WHO IS THE DEVIL?

HE'S THE RULER OF THIS WORLD

"And about judgment, because the (prince) ruler of this world has been judged." (John 16:11)

"I will not say much more to you, for the (prince) ruler of this world is coming. He has no hold over me, but he comes so that the world may learn." (John 14:30–31)

"As for you, you were dead when you followed the ways of this world, and of the ruler of the kingdom of the air (the prince of the power of the air), the spirit who is now at work in those who are disobedient." (Ephesians 2:1–2)

NEVER FORGET

When God threw Satan out of Heaven, he became ruler over the earth.

God gave him that position—but he can't just do whatever he wants.

He MUST obey within the framework of what God allows him within the four corners of God's Word—no more, no less—and this will remain true until the day of judgment.

THE POWER OF THE AIR

So, what's this "power of the air" that the enemy controls and is prince and ruler over?

The power of the air is influence.

By thought.

By talk.

By propaganda.

By lies.

By gaslighting, etc.

And, on the earth, there's no one better.

"You belong to your father, the devil, and you want to carry out your father's desires.

NOT HOLDING to the TRUTH, for there is NO TRUTH in him.

When HE LIES, HE SPEAKS HIS NATIVE LANGUAGE,

For HE is a LIAR and the FATHER of LIES." (John 8:44)

While the enemy does boom and blast his influence across all forms of communication—talk, gossip, TV, video, cable, radio, Internet, etc., he doesn't always want to make it booming or blasting.

Otherwise, we might catch on.

So, in addition, he does it by simple thoughts and quiet whispers. It's his version, or perversion, and the opposite of God's still small voice—kind of like the old picture of an angel on one shoulder and the devil on the other. In this case, the devil on the shoulder is more truth than fiction whispering in our ears all the time, trying to lead us astray, telling half-truths—whatever it takes to get us off course.

He doesn't care how he gets us off course or how few degrees off he can get us as long as he gets us there—by hook or by crook.

A SIMPLE ANALOGY

If you were flying a plane *BY INSTRUMENTATION ONLY* from LAX to LaGuardia and your instruments were off by only a few degrees, when you landed, you'd be in Miami International!

Hence, a few degrees off, over the long haul, will always get us way off course.

And the ruler of this world knows it.

TEMPTATION IN THE WILDERNESS

"Then Jesus was led by the Spirit into the wilderness to be tempted by the devil. After fasting forty days and forty nights, he was hungry.

The tempter came to him and said, 'If you are the Son of God, tell these stones to become bread.'

Jesus answered, 'It is written: Man shall not live on bread alone, but on every Word that comes from the Mouth of God.'

Then the devil took him to the holy city and had him stand on the highest point of the temple. 'If you are the Son of God', he said, 'throw yourself down. For it is written: He will command his angels concerning you, and they will lift you up in their hands, so that you will not strike your foot against a stone.'

Jesus answered him, 'It is also written: Do not put the Lord your God to the test.'

Again, the devil took him to a very high mountain and showed him all the kingdoms of the world and their splendor. 'All this I will give you,' he said, 'if you will bow down and worship me.'

Jesus said to him, 'Away from me, Satan!' For it is written: Worship the Lord your God, and serve Him only.'

Then the devil left Him, and angels came, and attended Him." (Matthew 4:1–11)

When the devil said, "For He will command His angels concerning you to guard you in all your ways; they will lift you up in their hands, so that you will not strike your foot against a stone," he was quoting Psalm 91:11–12.

Yes. The devil knows the scriptures—probably better than you or I ever will—but, per his normal, the devil wasn't throwing out audacious comments that the simpleminded could decipher. The devil told Jesus some truth mixed with some lies to try to make him fail.

He just perverted the truth by a few degrees here and there.

Jesus corrected him because the half-truth the devil said properly, "For He will command His angels concerning you," was intermixed with a lie: "If you cast yourself down."

Jesus could tell them apart.

Could we?

How about when we're exhausted?

How about when we're worn out?

How about after fasting for forty days?

DIFFERENTIATING

The enemy is very tricky. He's the ruler of this world. He'll set up all the circumstances around us to prepare us for failure—then he'll deploy his "air tactics."

So, how can we tell his air tactics apart from God's still small voice?

Number one is by knowing God's Word, but remember, that's not enough since the devil knows it also.

And, number two, by sensing if God's Peace that passes understanding is there in our hearts, confirming it or not—again, more later.

LAYERS AND LAYERS OF GASLIGHTING

Be on guard—at ALL times. Watch out for the many layers of gaslighting that will come at you through the power of the air—many, many, many different types of distractions.

Distractions on every side, even valid ones—ones that will try to keep your eyes focused away from the Lord.

GASLIGHTING IN THE CHURCH

Power.

Ego.

Control.

Fear.

Willing to do anything to gain acceptance.

Spirit-filled verses non-Spirit-filled.

Religiosity.

Fake spirituality.

Being under men's (or women's) "authority."

Fake faith.

Judgements, wrong praying, etc.

GASLIGHTING IN OUR LIVES

Temptation of every type of sin.

Fear.

Power.

Ego.

Control.

Money.

And many others.

There are legitimate things that we can and/or must do in life, but many of these same things can also be used as something to keep us from putting the Lord first.

THE ENEMY WORKS WITH WHATEVER WORKS ON YOU

Is it fear?

Is it lust?

Is it anger, hate, wrath?

Is it temptations for money, power or control?

Is it the desire to connect with the (wrong) spirits or spiritual realm?

He knows our weaknesses, and he will use it to his advantage.

HOW DOES HE KNOW WHAT WORKS ON YOU, ME, AND EVERYONE ELSE?

It's pretty simple, really.

As the ruler of this world, he and his demons have been running to and fro across the earth since the beginning of time—observing, gathering info, hoarding data, using it to control not only you but everyone around you.

Just imagine—since the enemy has been doing this for all time, they've gathered ALL information on EVERYONE who's ever lived or died. Consider it the LARGEST COMPUTER DATA BANK on everyone—EVER.

Bigger and more accurate than Google could EVER hope to become, smarter than the most imagined AI machine learning—EVER.

With all that data at their fingertips, can you see why psychics, spiritualists, spirit guides, fortune telling, seances, mystical religions, and the ilk might fool the masses? Accessing data from willing spirits who want to control you.

How about for ghost hunters and such? It's the same for those who go around "sensing" spirits, ghosts of the dead. These spirits can mimic and portray themselves as those ghosts, passing along the same data, using it to create "accurate manifestations."

This backing by the enemy is where these people get their "powers" by connecting and accessing current and past information that will, in turn, cause many to believe in them.

They can very accurately (100 percent) correctly tell you all the current info, whether information about you, those around you, and/or elsewhere, because they're watching over everyone and their every move.

They can very accurately (100 percent) correctly tell you about all the past because they were intimately observing and interacting with those others, including your dead relatives, trying to direct and control them but, no matter what, "documenting" their lives for future use.

Therefore, they can very accurately communicate to you as someone returning to you from "the other side," thereby playing a CON (confidence) GAME on you.

If they can accurately convince you about the current and past, then they can most likely get you under their control.

It's that (potential) 100 percent accuracy that fools most people.

Sidenote: Just another quick tangent. So why did I say "potential?"

You might notice that not all physics, and the ilk, have that "100 percent accurate" rating, reputation, or results—and might use that as an argument against what I'm saying—or at minimum cause you confusion here.

Well let's go back to the father of lies who's behind all this. In his sadistic twisted mind where he wants to control everybody and everything, he enjoys creating trouble, anxiety, confusion, and competition, even and especially, among his own "followers"—to see who can become the best at becoming his "worst of the worst"—to constantly, more deeply entrap and possess them "forever."

If he gave all those folks, yielding to his evil, *instant 100 percent accuracy*, then what's the fun in that? He'd rather make them work at it—forcing them to yield to (and worship) him and his (evil) "spirit guides"—making these folks more and more and uber dependent on him and his hordes to achieve their "powers." Therefore he forces them to compete to "earn" their way up the hierarchy.

Ok, I'm back.

So why do they save telling you the future until last?

Because when they try to predict the future, they're usually only about 50 percent right.

Why? Because they do NOT know the future.

They do know the current, so they can tell you all about you and your life or what someone you know might be doing at that moment, anywhere they are in the world, when the "reading" is happening. In such an instance, it seems like they might be telling the (very near) future, but the rest is just a fifty-fifty crap shoot—where they're making logical predictive guessing (like AI today) based on everyone's past histories and their vast "Google-type databases" of human nature reactions to predict future behaviors. Therefore, they will be right, probably 50 percent of the time.

They can EASILY DECEIVE THE MASSES when they are 100 percent correct about the current and the past. Then they will be given latitude for only 50 percent accurate future predictions, obtaining people's "buy in" by quoting "everyone has free will" and, therefore, "they might not listen to the spirits trying to guide them in the future."

Sounds pretty convincing, don't you think?

SO WHAT ABOUT THE PARANORMAL OR SUPERNATURAL?

As quoted from *The American Heritage Dictionary of the English Language*, fifth edition, *the paranormal* is defined as

1. Beyond the range of normal experience or scientific explanation.

2. Of or pertaining to parapsychology; pertaining to forces or mental processes, such as extrasensory perception or psychokinesis, outside the possibilities defined by natural or scientific laws, and

3. That which cannot be explained by scientific methods.

Therefore, the lingering question remains: Is the paranormal or supernatural from God, or is it from the enemy?

The answer is both.

The parts where we are touched by God directly, as I've described my experiences to this point, and more to come in upcoming chapters, are a definite YES.

The parts where we can discern, perceive, and sense God's direction, protection, insight, warnings, understanding, and other by the Holy Spirit are a definite YES.

The parts where we have legitimate interactions with God's angels are a definite YES. You will learn more about that in the upcoming chapter on "ANGELS."

But ALL the rest of the multitude of other paranormal and supernatural experiences are a definite NO.

They, once again, are deceptions directed by the ruler of this earth and his minions set up to distract us from the Truth and the true relationship with God and, thereby, lead us down the wrong path(s).

How will we know the difference?

By His Peace that passes understanding—again, more on that later.

RULING US FOR ALL TIME

The devil and his cohorts have been ruling and directing each and every one of us for all time.

The earth is their playground.

But what if we wholeheartedly 100 percent turned to the Lord? Yielded to Him? Got our life cleaned up and them out?

Then the enemy would lose his control over us, and he hates giving up control.

He'll do ANYTHING to get it back.

WHAT ARE HIS GOALS?

Controlling everyone on the earth so he can take us down to hell with him and his demons on the day of judgment—which he knows is coming—and because he's a sadist and the father of sadism, he enjoys inflicting pain on us.

He wants to keep us from the Father.

He wants to keep us in confusion.

He wants to keep us running from one thing to the next, from one end of the spectrum to the other. He really doesn't care what it is.

He doesn't care if its sin related.

He doesn't care if its religion related.

He doesn't care if it's some kind of spiritual perversion.

He doesn't care how many degrees off as long as it's anything but being 100 percent correct with the Lord.

He doesn't care if its good, bad, or ugly.

He doesn't care if you're an upstanding citizen or the scum of the earth.

He doesn't care if you're a Christian or a non-Christian.

He doesn't care if you're a white witch or a black witch.

He doesn't care if you're into white magic or black magic of any kind.

He wants to obtain direct control by sin or any means.

He wants to obtain direct control by getting you to yield to the wrong spiritual things—even in the churches—by adding just a little misdirection, by religion or religiosities, by "great spiritual" distractions, by denominations, by any offshoots, by any tangents, etc., no matter, here, there, and everywhere.

The enemy doesn't care what we do just as long as none of us stop, repent, and ask the Lord to come into our lives, giving over control, yielding to Him, allowing Him to clean up our lives and get rid of the oppressing, possessing, or other crap the enemy would like to do.

And worse, he'll panic if we learn to consistently yield ourselves to Christ, the Anointing, if we allow the Holy Spirit to flow through us and fill in all these areas, seeing rivers of living water flowing from our innermost being.

At which point, the enemy knows he's sunk, but rest assured, he will not quit. He will not take it lying down.

"Be alert and of sober mind. Your enemy the devil prowls around like a roaring lion looking for someone to devour." (1 Peter 5:8)

Consequently, he will try even harder and do anything to f— us up.

Just in case you notice and/or get tired of seeing it, I'm going to continue repeating and repeating "We're a vessel to whomever we yield."

WHY SO MUCH TIME?

You're probably wondering why in the hell I'm wasting so much time taking about the enemy. Isn't that giving him too much unnecessary attention?

No.

Two reasons:

First, you need to know your enemy—his strengths, his weakness, and his tactics—if you want to be able to defeat him.

And, second, if we don't learn from the past, we're doomed to repeat it.

While it should be obvious to some, stay away from witchcraft (white or black), magic (the same), occults, psychics, Ouija boards, tarot cards, fortune telling, spiritualists, spirit guides, seances, mystical religions, and every other kind of spiritual functions, teachings, actions, and any and all things that are not in the pureness of Christ Jesus and the one and only Holy Spirit.

All these other things will contain some degree of perversion by the prince of the power of the air. If you've done them already, then repent and ask the Lord to cleanse these areas in you.

CHAPTER SIX

IT'S A MATTER OF CHOICE AND YIELDING

"**I** F SERVING THE LORD seems undesirable to you, then CHOOSE for yourselves this day whom you will serve, whether the gods your ancestors served beyond the Euphrates, or the gods of the Amorites, in whose land you are living. But as for me and my household, (we CHOOSE) we will serve the Lord." (Joshua 24:15)

CHOICE AND YIELDING ARE A TRUISM IN EVERYTHING

Simply put, choice and yielding are the most important things we can do—EVER.

Choice and yielding are the ONLY powers you and I have in the spiritual realm. Did you hear that? The ONLY powers.

I'm sure many will disagree with me—again—but I don't care.

They'll say, "Don't we have power in prayer?"

"Don't we have power in praise and worship?"

"Don't we have power in fasting?"

"And with this manual, don't we have power in standing?"

Prayer, praise, worship, fasting, standing are all functions. They are actions. They have no power in themselves. We do those things in obedience as unworthy servants.

The only REAL POWER comes from God. That Power comes through when we choose God and His ways as we do these things and when we yield ourselves to God alone. Otherwise, ALL these actions are just meaningless "things."

When we choose and yield to Him, then He'll bring His Infinite Power to bear through those actions.

As I've continued to say to this point and will continue throughout this manual, always remember, "We're a vessel to whomever we yield."

You might get sick and tired of me repeating it, but it's one of the *MOST IMPORTANT* things I can ever pass on to you.

TWO GOLDEN PIPES

"Then the angel said to me, 'What do you see?' And I said, 'I see, and behold, a lampstand all of gold with its bowl on the top of it, and its seven lamps on it; also, two olive trees by it, one on the right side of the bowl, and the other on its left side.'

I said to the angel who was speaking with me, 'What are these, my lord?'

He said to me, 'This is the word of the Lord saying, NOT BY MIGHT nor BY POWER, but BY MY SPIRIT (MY ANOINTING), says the Lord of hosts.

Then I said to him, 'What are the two OLIVE TREES which are beside the two GOLDEN PIPES (VESSELS, CONDUITS, or CHANNELS), which empty the GOLDEN OIL from themselves?'

He said, 'These are the TWO (sources of) ANOINTINGS

[Again in the Hebrew, is 'yitshar' (yeets-hawr), which means, 'FRESH OIL', 'OIL', 'ANOINTED', 'ANOINTING'],

Who are Standing

[In the Hebrew, is 'amad' (aw-mad), which means, 'to take one's STAND', 'TO STAND']

By the Lord for the whole earth.'" (Zechariah 4:1–14)

While I'm sure many scholars could spend endless amount of time deciphering this scripture, I'm only concerned with one main part here.

In view of our earlier discussion, it's about being in CHRIST, the ANOINTING, the HOLY SPIRIT, and the OIL—the one and the same flowing from God through us to the earth.

Why TWO SOURCES that feed the Pipes, Vessels, or Channels?

Because God brings His Anointing to the world in two ways—directly from His throne via the Holy Spirit from the outside—and by rivers of living waters flowing from the innermost beings of yielded believers from the inside.

CATCH THE VISION

This is the analogy of us and our (ONLY) power.

We've been given the opportunity to be GOLDEN PIPES allowing GOLDEN OIL to flow from God through us to the earth from our innermost beings.

That's all we can do—choosing to let the OIL (the ANOINTING) flow through us as a PIPE, VESSEL, CONDUIT, CHANNEL for God. When we catch on to this, we will be able to see how little we can do in the spiritual realm yet how wonderful our function really is with God.

Once God created the earth, He set it up so nothing happens except by choice. He's not going to force anything upon us.

Jesus chose to come and die to redeem us.

We get to choose right from wrong.

We get to choose whatever we want to do or not do.

We get to choose, to yield to God or, in turn, consciously or unconsciously, choose to yield to the ruler of this world.

We can NOT manipulate or control God—EVER.

We are NOT in control—EVER.

We do NOT have the power—EVER—but we can choose and yield to the one who does. We can yield to His will.

If not, we're automatically yielding to the other.

In Luke 11:23, Jesus said,

"WHOEVER is NOT WITH ME is AGAINST ME, and whoever does not gather with me scatters."

Deuteronomy 13:6-8 says,

"If your very own brother, or your son or daughter, or the wife you love, or your closest friend secretly entices you, saying, 'Let us go and worship other gods'... DO NOT YIELD TO THEM or listen to them."

Here *YIELD* in the Hebrew is 'abah' (aw-baw), which means "to be willing," "consent," "obey," "want," "would accept," "YIELD," which equals "CHOICE."

In Joshua 24:21–23,

"Joshua said to the people, 'You are witnesses against yourselves that you have CHOSEN for yourselves the Lord, to serve Him.'

And they said, 'We are witnesses.'

'Now therefore, put away the foreign gods which are in your midst, and YIELD your hearts to the Lord, the God of Israel.'"

Here *YIELD* in the Hebrew is 'natah' (naw-taw), which means "incline," "stretch out," "bent down," "bowed," "offer," "turn aside," "turn away."

Therefore, when we YIELD to the Lord, His promises to us are:

"I, THE LORD, HAVE

- CALLED YOU IN (MY) RIGHTEOUSNESS

- I WILL TAKE HOLD OF YOUR HAND

- I WILL KEEP YOU

- AND WILL MAKE YOU TO BE A COVENANT FOR THE PEOPLE

- AND A LIGHT FOR THE GENTILES

- TO OPEN EYES THAT ARE BLIND

- TO FREE CAPTIVES FROM PRISON

- AND TO RELEASE FROM THE DUNGEON THOSE WHO SIT IN DARKNESS

I AM the Lord; that is my name!

I WILL NOT YIELD MY GLORY to another or My praise to idols." (Isaiah 42:6–8)

Let me repeat myself again.

We are VESSELS.

We have no power in ourselves, but we can allow the Fullness of the Godhead to flow through us.

Burn this into your mind:

"WE ARE A VESSEL TO WHOMEVER WE YIELD."

CHAPTER SEVEN

GOD CAN DO ANYTHING

AS ESTABLISHED, GOD IS INFINITE

GOD CREATED ALL BY THE WORD OF HIS MOUTH

"I N THE BEGINNING GOD created the heavens and the earth. The earth was formless and void, and darkness was over the surface of the deep, and the Spirit of God was moving over the surface of the waters.

Then God said, 'Let there be light';

And, there was light...

Then God said, 'Let there be an expanse in the midst of the waters, and let it separate the waters from the waters.';

And, it was so...

Then God said, 'Let the waters below the heavens be gathered into one place, and let the dry land appear';

And, it was so...

Then God said, 'Let the earth sprout vegetation: plants yielding seed, and fruit trees on the earth bearing fruit after their kind with seed in them';

And, it was so...

Then God said, 'Let there be lights in the expanse of the heavens to separate the day from the night, and let them be for signs and for seasons and for days and years; and let them be for lights in the expanse of the heavens to give light on the earth';

And, it was so...

Then God said, 'Let the waters teem with swarms of living creatures, and let birds fly above the earth in the open expanse of the heavens.'...

Then God said, 'Let the earth bring forth living creatures after their kind: cattle and creeping things and beasts of the earth after their kind';

And, it was so...

Then God said, 'Let Us make man in Our image, according to Our likeness'...

And, it was so." (Genesis 1:1–31)

GOD SAID IT, AND IT WAS SO.

GOD HOLDS ALL THINGS TOGETHER BY THE WORD OF HIS MOUTH

Psalm 33:6 tells us,

"By THE WORD of the LORD the heavens were made, and by THE BREATH of HIS MOUTH ALL their host."

And in Hebrews 1:3, we're told,

"The Son is the radiance of God's glory and the exact representation of His nature and being, sustaining and upholding ALL THINGS by THE WORD of HIS [MOUTH] POWER."

Power in the Greek is 'dunamis' (do-na-miss), meaning "power," "might," "strength—ability," "miracles," "miraculous powers."

ATOMS AND THEIR PARTICLES

Let's take a tangent and review some basic facts about atoms, then I'll explain why.

Protons, electrons, and neutrons are the atomic particles that make up the atom.

Atoms are microscopically tiny, but the atomic particles inside the atom are much smaller than that—so small, in fact, that science has determined that atoms are mostly composed of open space.

Protons have positive nuclear or magnetic power. All of them reside together in the center (nucleus) of the atom along with all neutrons.

Neutrons are neutral. They have no nuclear or magnetic power. Some scientists theorize that neutrons insulate protons, but that theory is unsubstantiated and easily challenged.

Electrons have negative nuclear or magnetic power, all flying in orbit around the nucleus. Atoms usually have an equal number of protons and electrons or, in the case when one electron has been added or removed, it's called an ion.

Electrons travel at the speed of light. Their size and distance are proportional to the planets orbiting around the sun.

That's a lot of open space.

The sun has an incredible magnetic force—so great, in fact, that it holds all the rotating planets in orbit.

In the same way, the magnetic power of the positive protons in the nucleus is equally as great—so substantial that it can hold the electrons in orbit.

This takes a tremendous amount of power especially when the electrons are traveling at the speed of light.

MAGNETIC FORCE

We're getting to the point, but for a moment, let's take another tangent—oh no, it's a double tangent! How will we be able to get back?

So let's talk magnetic force with the analogy of two magnets.

The first basic part of magnetic law—opposite forces attract.

The positive side of one magnet will immediately attract to the negative side of a second magnet.

Example: If you hold two magnets near each other, one's positive side near the other's negative side, they will immediately "snap" together.

The second basic part of magnetic law—like forces repel (push apart).

The positive side of one magnet will immediately push away from the positive side of a second magnet. As well as, the reverse is true. The negative side of one magnet will immediately push away from the negative side of a second magnet.

Example: If you hold two magnets near each other, positive to positive or negative to negative, they will immediately "jump" or "fly" apart from each other.

SO BACK TO ATOMS

The magnetic force of protons, all huddled together in the nucleus, is so powerful that it holds all electrons in orbit—electrons flying at the speed of light and proportionally at the distance of the planets from the sun.

That type of magnetic force is monumental—massive, enormous, immense, overwhelmingly powerful.

So, the big question: If protons are ALL POSITIVELY CHARGED, ALL HUDDLED TOGETHER in the NUCLEUS, then why don't the protons "blow" apart from each other?

By all science, understanding magnetic forces, they should!

What holds them together? Neutrons?

Nope.

No science validates that theory.

That's just not what they do. They just don't have enough insulating capability to do that, and because the atomic particles are so small, proportionally, having so much open space between them, that would never work.

Then what does hold them together?

Bottom line: Science just doesn't know.

Science cannot address nor explain why.

So, they insert theories about "unknown" particles.

SO, WHAT DOES?

The Word of God.

The Word of His Mouth as spoken by Him in Genesis.

You say, "WHAT?"

Yes, God holds everything together by the Word of His Mouth.

God defies (or goes beyond) science—because God made science.

WHAT IF GOD DIDN'T HOLD THEM TOGETHER?

If God didn't hold the atoms together, they'd blow apart as all magnetic science denotes they should.

Then what would happen? Every atom's proton's overwhelming positive magnetic force would cause them to repel, disperse, and fly far away from each other.

Therefore, with the nucleus dispersed, the electrons and neutrons would just float away—having nothing to hold them in place.

As the protons dispersed, each individual proton's positive magnetic force would attract one floating electron—that would then fly in orbit around that proton, creating a new atom.

What type atom would you end up with, when you have one proton and one electron? Hydrogen—hydrogen gas.

What did Genesis 1 say? "The earth was formless and void."

Many scientists theorize it may've been a bunch of hydrogen gas floating around before they say the "big bang theory" happened.

Hydrogen gas—again.

Getting the connection yet?

Do you want to know what the "big bang theory" really is?

THEN GOD SAID, "... LET THERE BE ...", AND IT WAS SO

And from the hydrogen gas was formed every kind of atom—that then formed everything else. Pretty amazing, if you take the time to let that sink in!

What's more amazing is that it's STILL ALL HELD TOGETHER by the Word of His Mouth!

If not, we already know that EVERYTHING WOULD FLY APART and RETURN to HYDROGEN GAS.

So for those of us who've ever wondered or doubted if God is really here, really cares, is really in charge, or can really do the things the Bible says He can do, then just stop and think.

If He did not hold you, me, everyone, and everything in this world together, we'd just be a bunch of gas—and science proves it.

If that doesn't amaze you, I just don't know what would.

A SPARROW FALLS

So when God says He knows when a sparrow falls and that He has all the hairs numbered on your head, He does.

"Are not two sparrows sold for a penny? Yet not one of them will fall to the ground without your Father's notice and consent. And, even the very hairs of your head are all numbered. So, don't be afraid; you are worth more than many sparrows." (Matthew 10:29–31)

ANOTHER TANGENT

Back in the day, I had a lot of long thick hair. I've always been very vain about my hair, always brushing or combing throughout the day to keep it looking good. Unfortunately, it's not so long or thick anymore as time has passed and taken its toll, but I'm still vain on how it looks and comb often.

Then one day, per my daily routine, I was vainly staring into the mirror, combing my good-looking locks. As I did, I'd stop along the way, pull the hairs from the comb, and throw them into the trash then repeat the process over and over until all looked perfect.

In the middle of that routine, the Lord calmly asked, "What ya doing?"

Thinking it was pretty obvious, I replied, "Combing my hair, grabbing the hairs from the comb, and throwing them in the trash," and went back at it.

A couple minutes later, the Lord calmly asked me again, "What ya doing?"

Wondering why He repeated this "silly" question. I replied again, "Combing my hair, grabbing the hairs from the comb, and throwing them in the trash," and again went back to it.

For a third time, the Lord calmly asked, "What ya doing?"

Now rolling my eyes, starting to get annoyed, I responded with disdain, "Obviously combing my hair, grabbing the hairs from the comb, and throwing them in the trash. Why do you keep asking me!"

He said, "But do you really know what you're doing?"

Kinda pissed, now with an attitude, I said, "Yeah! Just combing my hair, grabbing the hairs from the comb, and throwing them in the trash! Why, what do you think I'm doing?"

He said, "Did you know that you just threw hair number 8,253, hair number 50,812, hair number 915, and hair number 22,601 in the trash?"

I STOOD THERE IN SHOCK.

At that moment, I realized He cared more about me than I cared about myself.

The God of the universe watches and cares about every single one of the fifty-thousand (plus or minus) hairs on top of everyone's head across the world—every moment of every day.

If He does that, can't we trust Him to look out for our best interests?

And while that's amazing by itself, it's still minor compared to the fact that He holds every atom together inside you, me, everyone, animals, plants, waters, skies, and everything else—ALL BY THE WORD OF HIS MOUTH!

NOW THAT'S BEYOND AMAZING!

CHAPTER EIGHT

AUTHORITY IN CONJUNCTION WITH THE WILL OF GOD

LET'S TALK AUTHORITY

JESUS DRIVES OUT AN IMPURE SPIRIT

"ON THE SABBATH HE taught the people. They were amazed at His teaching, because HIS WORDS HAD AUTHORITY.

In the synagogue there was a man possessed by demon(s), impure spirit(s); he cried out at the top of his voice, 'Go away! What do you want with us, Jesus of Nazareth? Have you come to destroy us? I know who you are—the Holy One of God!'

'Be quiet!' Jesus said sternly. 'Come out of him!' Then the demon(s) threw the man down before them all and came out without injuring him.

All the people were amazed and said to each other, 'What words these are! With AUTHORITY and POWER, He gives orders to impure spirits and they come out!'" (Luke 4:31–36)

FAITH AS SMALL AS A MUSTARD SEED

"A man approached Jesus and knelt before Him. 'Lord, have mercy on my son,' he said. 'He has seizures and is suffering greatly. He often falls into the fire or into the water.

I brought him to your disciples, but they could not heal him.'

'You unbelieving and perverse generation,' Jesus replied, 'how long shall I stay with you? How long shall I put up with you? Bring the boy here to me.'

Jesus REBUKED the DEMON, and IT CAME OUT of the BOY, and HE WAS HEALED at that moment.

Then the disciples came to Jesus in private and asked, 'Why couldn't we drive it out?'

He replied, 'Because you have so little faith. Truly I tell you, if you have faith as small as a mustard seed, you can say to this mountain, move from here to there, and it will move.'

Nothing will be impossible for you." (Matthew 9:14–20)

AUTHORITY OVER THE WIND

Jesus was asleep in the disciples' boat when the disciples woke Him out of fear since a terrible storm had arisen.

"He got up, rebuked the wind and said to the waves, 'Quiet! Be still!' Then the wind died down, and it was completely calm.

He said to his disciples, 'Why are you so afraid? Do you still have no faith?'

They were terrified and asked each other, 'Who is this? Even the WIND and the WAVES OBEY HIM!" (Mark 4:39–41)

YOU MUST BE IN GOD'S WILL

Back in the day, a group of maybe fifty people from our church went out to a park area with a pond with plans to have a baptism and then picnic together.

The weather was supposed to be nice, and it was a warm, beautiful, sunny afternoon there.

Then all of a sudden, the weather turned bad.

The skies became full of black storm clouds. The wind kicked up. Soon it turned into blasting gusts, blowing everything off the ground and picnic tables.

It looked hopeless. The baptism and picnic were over.

Most of the group gathered up what the wind hadn't already blown away and ran for their cars, yet a few of us stayed.

We stood up on a picnic table.

We stared into the menacing swelling black storm clouds and gusting winds, and we began praying for several long minutes, then simultaneously, we all stopped and commanded the wind,

"Peace, be still"—nothing more.

Immediately, just as quickly as the storm had blown in, it dissipated.

The wind was calm.

The sun broke through the clouds and shone brightly again, and a beautiful sunset displayed across the skies.

All who had rushed for their cars came back.

We continued with the baptism and picnic.

Note: That use of Authority can only be done in faith, in God's will and in God's timing. It cannot be done UNLESS it's what the Father wants. Therefore, we must have His (current release of) faith knowing we're in His will and His timing.

TORNADO AND THE CHURCH

As I said previously, we had meetings almost every night and some days twice.

One Wednesday night, we were all gathered for a service at our local church. It was one of the hubs where the Holy Spirit was manifesting greatly during the early Charismatic move.

We were in the midst of a very loud intense worship service—nothing unusual about that—not in any rush to do anything. In those days, we didn't do a bunch of preplanned music with a bunch of song leaders, as is done nowadays, so the normal, unscripted, unprepared worship, without limits, could easily last for hours.

In the middle of this worship, we began to hear torrential rain beating on the roof, the sides, and the windows of the building. It got louder and louder. Eventually, it got so loud that it sounded like a roaring freight train overhead.

We didn't stop.

It got louder.

We got louder.

The worst of the storm lasted for maybe a half hour or so.

It wasn't until hours later, when we got home, that some of the members who hadn't gone to the service that night called. They said, "Did you see the tornado?"

We said, "No, but we sure heard something extremely loud."

"Did it pass nearby?"

AS SEEN ON LOCAL TV WEATHER COVERAGE

They said, "You won't believe it. We wouldn't have believed it if we hadn't seen it with our own eyes. We were watching the local news, tracking and broadcasting the weather as a very large black funnel cloud (a severe tornado) was coming down the freeway, tearing up everything in its path."

That freeway passed right next to the church.

"When it got in line with the church, like it had a mind of its own, it turned ninety degrees from the freeway, directly into the path of the church, then continued its destruction.

"We watched as the bottom of the funnel touched the ground along the way, tearing up all in its path. When it reached just outside the church property, it came to a dead stop. It hesitated for several very long moments.

"At which point, the whole tornado rose straight up in the air with its bottom now higher than the top of the steeple. It did this without any other movement, at which point, it started moving again very slowly, directly over the top of the church.

"When it got to the other side of the church parking area, it hesitated, stopping again. After a few more long moments, the bottom of the funnel descended back to earth. Once again, it started moving, tearing up all in its path."

The church, the people, the cars, and all were completely untouched.

We said, "That must've been happening when we heard the deafening sound of a freight train." Yes, God still does miracles for His people.

Note: We didn't need to know the details—actually, no one ever needs to know the all details—no one needed to say or do something "special." Authority came through yielding to the Lord as we worshipped Him.

BACK TO MOVING THE MOUNTAIN TO THE SEA

"Jesus answered. 'Truly I tell you, if anyone says to this mountain, Go, throw yourself into the sea, and does not doubt in their heart but believes that what they say will happen, it will be done for them.'" (Mark 11:22–23)

Sending the mountain into the sea is a lesson on faith when under God's Authority, and Jesus said we could do that—right?

BUT did Jesus ever tell a mountain to move to the sea?

EVER?

NO.

Why?

Because the Father NEVER told Him to do so.

Therefore, it's not an issue of just having faith with Authority. It's always been a matter of God's will being done while under His Authority.

Not our will—not our authority.

DID JESUS HEAL THEM ALL?

We know that He did numerous times in the gospels such as in Luke 6:17 where,

"Jesus came down with them; and, there was a large crowd who had come to hear Him,

To be healed of their diseases;

And, those who were troubled with unclean spirits were being cured.

All the people were trying to touch Him,

For POWER was COMING FROM HIM, and HEALING THEM ALL."

But was that always the case?

At the pool at Bethesda, in John 5:2–9, it says,

"Now there is in Jerusalem, by the sheep gate, a pool, which is called in Hebrew, Bethesda, having five porches. In these lay a multitude of those who were sick, blind, lame, and withered,

Waiting for the moving of the waters; [for an angel of the Lord went down at certain seasons into the pool and stirred up the water; whoever then first, after the stirring up of the water, stepped in was made well from whatever disease with which he was afflicted.]

A man was there who had been ill for thirty-eight years.

When Jesus saw him lying there, and knew that he had already been a long time in that condition, He said to him, 'Do you wish to get well?'

The sick man answered Him, 'Sir, I have no man to put me into the pool when the water is stirred up, but while I am coming, another steps down before me.'

Jesus said to him, 'Get up, pick up your pallet and walk.'

IMMEDIATELY, the MAN BECAME WELL, and picked up his pallet, and began to walk."

Now, that is wonderful! But, have you ever taken the time to really consider what happened here?

Jesus walked through the five porches, stepping over and around many, many, many sick people and on that day went up to only one person and healed him—alone.

Why did Jesus only heal one that day?

Why didn't Jesus heal them all?

Didn't he care for all of them?

Simply because that was God's will for that time and place—to heal one and only one.

The lesson to be learned here: It's not our faith or what we want or when we want it.

It's what God the Father wants when He wants it.

We, too, will have Authority if we are under God's Authority and when we're doing the will of the Father.

You don't need to ask if you have Authority. Either you know you're under God's Authority and you have it—or not.

THE COP AND THE CROSSROADS

There's a story I was told about very small crossroads town nestled in a valley between two steep hills.

There was only one main road that ran in and out, passing between the two hills through the little town.

Every day at noon, a large semi-truck zoomed down one hill, blasting through the town in order to get a good run up the other hill.

The townspeople were terrified by the truck, afraid their children or themselves would be mowed down, so every day at noon, they would be seen jumping out of its way.

Now there was only one sheriff for the town.

At noon, you could find him eating lunch at the only diner there.

Daily—the town's people badgered him—why he didn't put a stop to the semi-truck terrifying their safety? It was such a small town, and because everyone knew he was the sheriff he always dressed in plain clothes along with his fellow townspeople. He did not feel the need to dress differently.

Finally, one day, he gave in to their incessant pestering.

He really didn't know what he could do to stop the truck, but he walked outside into the middle of the road.

As the semi started its descent into town, the sheriff raised his arm, hand and fingers extended, and yelled, "STOP!"

Per normal, the semi barreled through town. It didn't slow down in the least. It would've run the sheriff over if he hadn't leaped out of the way in the nick of time.

NOW the sheriff was PISSED and determined to stop the truck!

The following day, he went out in full uniform with his badge in clear display on his chest.

Again, at noon, the truck barreled through town.

Now, for a second time, the sheriff stood in the middle of the road. Again, he raised his arm, hand up and extended, and yelled, "STOP!"

This time brakes squealing, wheels smoking—the semi came to a screeching halt—just inches from running over the sheriff.

Why did the uncaring driver stop this time?

Was the sheriff a different man?

Did he say or do anything differently than he had done the day before?

NO.

The difference this time was he was cloaked in his uniform and badge.

The sheriff could now be clearly seen for who he was and representing all the authorities behind him.

The semi driver didn't comply because he was fearful of the man. He knew the man couldn't stop a rushing semi.

Instead, the semi driver was fearful of the authorities behind the man.

He understood that if he didn't stop, he'd not only have the city authorities after him but also the county authorities, the state authorities, and the full weight of the federal authorities after him.

HE HAD TO COMPLY, OR IT WOULD'VE BEEN THE END OF HIM.

BY THE WORD, WE WERE GIVEN ALL AUTHORITY OVER ALL THE ENEMY

In Luke 10:17-20,

"The seventy-two returned with joy and said, 'Lord, even the demons submit to us in your name.'

He replied, 'I saw Satan fall like lightning from heaven.

I HAVE GIVEN YOU AUTHORITY to trample on snakes, and scorpions, and OVER ALL THE POWER of the ENEMY;

NOTHING WILL HARM YOU.

However, do not rejoice that the spirits submit to you, but rejoice that your names are written in heaven.'"

So why does the enemy have to obey us?

I absolutely guarantee the enemy is NOT afraid of us, but when we're wearing God's "uniform" and "badge," they're afraid of the one who backs us.

Remember, they know the Word better than we do.

They know when we're under God's Authority and standing in His Word, if they don't obey, they will be destroyed, annihilated, demolished by God.

WHAT WOULD I DO DIFFERENTLY?

So how would I handle the tiny small voice in my ear differently today?

Whether I might've made the initial mistake to yield and listen or not, I'd bind the enemy, command them to be quiet, and then leave—in the Name of Jesus—followed by loosing the Holy Spirit to come backfill the void.

No antics, no drama, no yelling, and no sending the poor dog out the door!

CHAPTER NINE

JUDGMENT

JUDGE, JUDGING, AND JUDGMENT

THE GREEK HAS MANY words for *judge, judging, and judgment.*

They range from simple decisions to discernment to acting as a final judge in God's white throne judgment. In between are many levels—from making an evaluation, distinguishing the truth, deciding right from wrong, or closely examining your own or others' actions.

We've all heard the scripture "Judge not, lest you be judged" from the book of Matthew.

Is that true for all types of judgment?

Are we to NOT judge at all? Or which one is He talking about?

Let's quickly look at some of the different types of judgment.

"TO JUDGE" EQUALS "TO DISCERN"

"And this I pray, that your love may abound still more and more in REAL KNOWLEDGE and ALL JUDGEMENT (DISCERNMENT), so that you may APPROVE the things that are EXCELLENT, in order to be sincere and blameless until the day of Christ." (Philippians 1:9–10)

Discernment is about being able to clearly understand what God is saying, what people around you are saying, what the things around you are telling you, what the spiritual realm around you is doing.

Discernment IS A GOOD THING.

"TO JUDGE" EQUALS "TO EXAMINE OURSELVES"

Concerning partaking in communion, we're told,

"So then, whoever eats the bread or drinks the cup of the Lord in an unworthy manner will be guilty of sinning against the Body and Blood of the Lord.

EVERYONE ought to EXAMINE (JUDGE) THEMSELVES, before they eat of the bread and drink from the cup. For those who eat and drink, WITHOUT DISCERNING the Body of Christ, EAT and DRINK JUDGMENT on themselves.

That is why many among you are weak and sick, and a number of you have fallen asleep. But, if we were MORE DISCERNING with REGARD to OURSELVES, we would NOT COME UNDER SUCH JUDGMENT.

Nevertheless, when we are judged in this way by the Lord, we are being disciplined so that we will not be finally condemned with the world." (1 Corinthians 11:27–32)

Examining ourselves, examining our motives, examining our actions, and doing the same for other people CAN BE A GOOD THING.

As it says, we must become more discerning with regard to ourselves, inasmuch, before eating the bread and drinking from the cup, which represents the Body and Blood. We must examine how we perceive, JUDGE, the Body of Christ, or we will end up being judged by God.

This is another one of those NEGATIVE statements.

To better understand the error in those judgments, see the army of God, below.

"TO JUDGE" EQUALS "TO DECIDE RIGHT FROM WRONG"

"So, give Your servant an understanding heart to JUDGE [GOVERN] your people to DISCERN [DECIDE] between RIGHT and WRONG. For who is able to JUDGE [GOVERN] this great people of Yours?" (1 Kings 3:9)

Deciding, judging, right from wrong, once again, CAN BE A GOOD THING.

Pretty obvious—not much more needs to be said here.

"TO JUDGE" EQUALS "TO DISTINGUISH GOOD FROM EVIL"

"But solid food is for the mature, who by constant use have trained themselves to JUDGE [DISTINGUISH] GOOD from EVIL." (Hebrews 5:14)

Distinguishing, judging, good from evil is ABSOLUTELY NECESSARY FOR OUR LIVES.

Once again, not much more needs to be said.

"TO JUDGE" EQUALS "TO BE EXPOSED BY THE LIGHT AND THE TRUTH"

Concerning Light:

"This is the message we have heard from Him and announce to you, that GOD is LIGHT, and in Him there is NO DARKNESS at all." (1 John 1:5)

"Then Jesus again spoke to them, saying, 'I AM the LIGHT of the world; he who follows Me WILL NOT WALK in the DARKNESS, but will have the LIGHT of LIFE.'" (John 8:12)

LIGHT and sunlight expose darkness. LIGHT judges darkness. LIGHT causes darkness to flee at the speed of light.

Concerning Truth:

As stated previously from John 8:44,

"You belong to your father, the devil, and you want to carry out your father's desires.

NOT HOLDING to the TRUTH, for there is NO TRUTH in him.

When HE LIES, HE SPEAKS HIS NATIVE LANGUAGE,

For HE is a LIAR and the FATHER of LIES."

And in John 8:32,

"Then you will know the TRUTH, and the TRUTH will set you free [from ALL the lies from the FATHER of LIES]."

Lies, including ALL propaganda and gaslighting, are the OPPOSITE of the TRUTH. The TRUTH REVEALS and EXPOSES ALL lies.

EXPOSING ALL DARKNESS AND ALL LIES ARE A VERY GOOD THING.

THE WRONG JUDGEMENT: "TO JUDGE" EQUALS "JUDGING OTHERS"

I don't know about you, but I've f—ed up a LOT in this area—and still do.

I judge a LOT.

But I'm sure I'm the only one.

Right?

My first marriage was horrible. I call my ex the "Queen of B's." While there were a few good years and four good children, to me, with all the incessant mental, physical, and physiological hell she put me through, she was. Yet with as much horrid pain and anguish she plagued my life for many years, I do NOT have the right to judge her character that way.

I do have every right to say I hate the things she did to me and the evil behind it yet not hate her or wish evil upon her by judging her character that way.

Then there are all the people doing stupid things that piss me off a lot of the time and in a lot of ways. Take drivers for example.

Again, I'm sure that I'm the only one here who does this.

When the f—ing idiots don't know how to drive or pull some kind of a$$hole stunt, I give them the finger and tell them what I think. They're just "bonehead dumb $hits."

No, I don't like their actions; and no, I don't have to like them personally, but I'm not allowed to pronounce that kind of character judgment on them.

I'm allowed to say, "I'm pissed" and "I feel like they did 'this and that' stupid a$$ or bonehead thing"; but not the "You're a worthless piece of $hit" or the "You're a f—ing bonehead idiot" judgments.

Once again, I'm sure I'm the only one who does anything like this when I'm angry—not you, just me—but again I digress.

Ephesians 4:26–27 says,

"Be ANGRY, and yet DO NOT SIN; do not let the sun go down on your anger, and do not give the devil an opportunity."

As I said, I f— up a LOT in this area.

Hey, I might not be good in this area, but at least I am truthful.

Sometimes it takes a bit before the Holy Spirit gets my attention and lets me know that I'm doing wrong—then I usually wrestle with the fact that I don't really want to do what He wants 'cause I'm mad—then in a bit, I repent and define (redefine) it correctly, without the judgment.

Remember the game of "hot potato" we played as kids? This should be a "hot potato" that we throw away as fast as we can.

Unfortunately, I'm not too good at this one.

I'm a bit slow, maybe "a bit thick" sometimes. I'm sure many would agree.

"DO NOT JUDGE, or YOU TOO will be JUDGED. For in the SAME WAY YOU JUDGE OTHERS, YOU will be JUDGED, and with the measure you use, it will be measured to you.

Why do you look at the speck of sawdust in your brother's eye and pay no attention to the log in your own eye? How can you say to your brother, 'Let me take the speck out of your eye,' when all the time there is a log in your own eye?

You hypocrite, first take the log out of your own eye, and then you will see clearly to remove the speck from your brother's eye." (Matthew 7:1–5)

Here the word *JUDGE* is the Greek word, 'krinō' (kree-no), which means to "act as judge," "condemn," "pass judgment," "as to law," "stand trial."

It's identical to how God will judge us.

This same Greek, 'krinō', is used in Revelations 20:11–12:

"Then I saw a great white throne, and Him who was seated on it. The earth and the heavens fled from His Presence, and there was no place for them. And I saw the dead, great and small, standing before the throne, and books were opened.

Another book was opened, which is the book of life. The DEAD WERE JUDGED ['krinō'] according to what they had done as recorded in the books."

Hence, this is the kind of judgment we're NOT supposed to do—God's type of judgment, 'Krinō', especially when judging people's character—but we do.

If you want to have Authority, you must get rid of this type judgment in your life; and in the chapter on Blessing and Cursing, we'll see that this judgment is also a dangerous issue of the heart.

HOW ABOUT CHRISTIANS?

In case you haven't figured this out yet, Christians are the worst.

YES.

I mean us—ALL of us.

Dick used to say to me "Christians are the only army that shoot their wounded."

We can be the nastiest, vilest, foulest, wickedest.

We judge others.

We condemn them for their sins.

Even though we have our own [such hypocrites].

Then expel them from our midst.

It should not be so. We need to be different.

"Then let us NO LONGER, CRITICIZE, and BLAME, and PASS JUDGMENT ['krinō'] on one another,

But rather decide and endeavor NEVER to PUT a STUMBLING BLOCK or an OBSTACLE or a HINDRANCE in the way of a brother." (Romans 14:13)

Yet many will state, in their defense and as their justified religious excuse, that they were given full permission to so based on First Corinthians 5:11-13—where "they were told to do it."

"But actually, I wrote to you not to associate with any so-called brother if he is an immoral person, or covetous, or an idolater, or a reviler, or a drunkard, or a swindler—not even to eat with such a one. For what have I to do with judging ['krinō'] outsiders? Do you not judge ['krinō'] those who are within the church? But those who are outside, God judges ['krinō']. *Remove the wicked man from among yourselves.*"

Remove in the Greek is a combination of three words 'exairō' (ex-air-oo), 'ek' (eck), and 'airō' (air-oo). It can mean 'remove', but also Exairō means to 'lift up', as well as, 'to remove'. Ek means 'from out of', 'based', 'belonging', 'depends', 'grudgingly', 'heavenly', 'reason', 'under [the glove]', 'through'. And 'airō' means 'to raise [up]', 'take up', 'lift [up]', 'lifted', 'hoisted', 'picked [up]', 'bear [up]'.

Wicked and *man* in the Greek are the same word 'ponēros' (po-nay-roo-tee-ros) from 'poneō' (po-knee-o), which can mean 'wicked man', but also means 'to toil', 'toilsome', 'evil', 'wicked things'.

Yourselves in the Greek is a combination of two words 'su' (soo) and 'autos' (ow-tos), which can mean 'yourselves', but also means 'like-minded', 'self', 'agree', 'personally', 'together', 'temple', 'righteousness', 'these things', 'together'.

So instead of interpreting it as

"Remove the wicked man from among yourselves"

it could easily be read as

"To lift (him) up from out of (his) sin [with the heavenly reason and intent and from under the glove (in submission to God)] to raise (him) up from the toilsome, evil, and wicked things from the like-minded".

Also, did you catch the context before it? It says "Do you not judge ['krinō'] those who are within the church?". He NEVER said we should 'krinō' them, He asked don't we already 'krinō' them? So unfortunately, once again, per our normal, we're doing it wrong.

BOTTOM LINE:

God does NOT want us pronouncing 'krinō' on them. He NEVER said we could. He NEVER gave us permission or justification to do so—simply because our intent (always) STINKS—therefore we are NEVER allowed to 'krinō' anyone anytime for any reason.

Now when you see it as **"To lift (him) up from out of (his) sin [with the heavenly reason and intent and from under the glove (in submission to God)] to raise (him) up from the toilsome, evil, and wicked things from the like-minded"**;

Are you able to see the difference from our flawed intent of us 'krinō'ing them to God's *Pure Intent of Redemption?*

CHAPTER TEN

THE SECRET OF HUMILITY

HUMILITY IS PRETTY STRAIGHT FORWARD, THE SECRET IS NOT

T HE BASIC UNDERSTANDING OF humility should be self-evident and straight forward. Therefore, let's allow the scriptures to speak for themselves.

"The MEEK [the HUMBLE] shall inherit the earth and shall delight themselves in the abundance of Peace." (Psalm 37:11)

"This is the man to whom I will look and have regard: he who is HUMBLE and of a BROKEN or WOUNDED SPIRIT, and WHO TREMBLES at My WORD and REVERES My COMMANDS." (Isaiah 66:2)

"When pride comes, then comes dishonor, but with the HUMBLE, is WISDOM. (Proverbs 11:2)

"A man's pride will bring him low, but he who is of a HUMBLE SPIRIT will obtain honor." (Proverbs 29:23)

"Take my yoke upon you and learn from me, for I AM GENTLE and HUMBLE in HEART, and you will find rest for your souls." (Matthew 11:29)

Hopefully, it's pretty obvious to this point.

"And ALL of you, CLOTHE YOURSELVES with HUMILITY toward one another, for GOD is OPPOSED to the PROUD, but GIVES GRACE to the HUMBLE." (1 Peter 5:5)

SO WHAT'S NEW?

You say, "Humility is not some new, great revelation. So, what's the big secret here?" Good question. Glad you asked.

Let's look at a verse often used in teaching spiritual warfare—James 4:7.

Many times, it's simply quoted,

"Resist the devil, and he will flee from you."

Sometimes it's quoted with the whole verse, adding in,

"Submit yourselves to God, resist the devil, and he will flee from you."

Submit in the Greek is 'hupotassō' (hoop-ot-as-so), which means "to place or rank under," "to subject," "to obey," "put in subjection," "subjected," "subjecting," "submissive," "submit." Which is from the prim root 'hupo' (hoop-o), which means "by," "under," "about," "hands," "under: power."

So a simple view of *submission* from the Greek means "to put the hand inside or under [the glove]." Looking back at Authority, we've determined we must put ourselves inside or under God's Authority to have Authority.

All good stuff, and that we MUST do—but that's still not the secret.

So what is?

99

Few, if any, teach it in context to the verse before it. Verse 6 states (just as in First Peter 5:5),

"GOD is OPPOSED to the PROUD but GIVES GRACE to the HUMBLE."

If you don't add humility into the mix, it just won't work.

SO, THE SECRET TO MAKING THE ENEMY FLEE

We must resist the devil.

But before that, we must submit ourselves to God.

But before that, we must humble ourselves before God.

To say it in proper order:

Humble yourself.

Then submit yourself.

Then resist.

And then, the enemy will flee.

BOTTOM LINE

If you want to operate in the Authority God gave us over the enemy, you MUST FIRST and ALWAYS HUMBLE YOURSELF before God.

REMEMBER CANCER?

God miraculously healed my cancer at seventeen years old, but nowadays—or more like now-a-years—I'm going through a bunch of physical problems: back, hip, knee surgeries, CHF, and prostate cancer.

I guess God, being God, does what He wants when He wants.

We can't tell Him what to do. He's not a "genie in a bottle" that we can rub (with our faith) in the right way, and He'll "give us three wishes."

On the contrary, we can only believe (exercise the faith He gives) when He says He's going to do something.

Otherwise, I guess myself, along with many, are just being humbled—like it or not.

APOSTLE PAUL

He certainly was one of greatest, most yielded believers ever recorded, yet,

"To keep me from exalting myself, there was given me a thorn in the flesh, a messenger of Satan to torment me.

Concerning this I implored the Lord three times that it might leave me. And He has said to me, 'My Grace is sufficient for you, for Power is perfected in weakness.'

Most gladly, therefore, I will rather boast about my weaknesses, so that the Power of CHRIST (the ANOINTING) may dwell in me.

Therefore, I am well content with weaknesses, with insults, with distresses, with persecutions, with difficulties,

For CHRIST's [the ANOINTING's] sake; for when I am weak, then I am strong." (2 Corinthians 12:7–10)

If God humbled Paul, then rest assured He'll do the same for us.

Therefore, CHOOSE HUMILITY.

If you don't, God will CHOOSE it for you.

Remember this lesson when we talk about Dick and the "Blue Devils" a bit later.

CHAPTER ELEVEN

BE "ON GUARD," STAY VIGILANT

THE "ROARING LION" EFFECT

THE ENEMY'S FIRST STRATEGY is to act as a roaring lion—to scare the $hit out of you.

"Be alert, well balanced [temperate, of sober mind], be vigilant and cautious at all times. Because your enemy, the devil, PROWLS AROUND like a ROARING LION looking for SOMEONE to DEVOUR." (1 Peter 5:8)

"Now there was a day when the sons of God came to present themselves before the Lord, and Satan also came among them. The Lord said to Satan, 'From where do you come?' Then Satan answered the Lord and said, 'From roaming about on the earth and walking around on it.'" (Job 1:6–7)

The enemy roams to and fro, across the earth, roaring like a lion, looking for easy prey.

If a lion really wanted to capture and kill their prey, they would NOT roar. They'd stalk, very quietly sneaking up on their prey. When close enough, they'd run and pounce to capture and kill.

Then, why would a lion want to roar?

Either they want to show dominance, or they want to scare everything and everyone away then take a nap.

Understanding this, then why would the devil want to be a roaring lion verses a stalking lion? SIMPLY, to invoke fear.

Back in the day—yes, those same Charismatic days—as we gathered one night in our homegroup—someone had a vision worth sharing.

He was watching as a massive dreadful lion approached, threatening and roaring. He was frozen in place. He was paralyzed with fear. He could not move, waiting for annihilation.

He watched as the lion got closer and closer.

He was terrified.

Eventually, the lion reached him—then, passed by—continuing on.

Somewhat calming down from his fear—he saw something amazing on the back side of the lion. It was actually just a cardboard cutout with a lion painting on the front attached to a bicycle.

On the bike was a skinny, scrawny man frantically pedaling away. As he pedaled, he was carrying a megaphone and imitating "vicious roars."

What's the moral to this vision?

That if we yield ourselves to the Lord and STAND in His strength, we'll see that even the scariest "fifty-foot-tall lion" is nothing to fear.

FALLING FOR THE THINGS THAT WILL TAKE US DOWN

If fear doesn't work, look for distractions—any kind, from any direction, at any level.

Remember, he just needs to get us off by a few degrees.

So what are "the things that will take us down"?

Temptation of every type of sin.

Pride.

Power.

Ego.

Control.

Lust.

(Misuse of) Sex.

(Worshipping) Money.

Anger, Hate, Wrath.

Falling for "religion" or religiosity (false religions).

Or the opposite—no religion (remembering that TRUE RELIGION is looking after orphans and widows [James 1:27]).

Falling for anything that will take our eyes off the Lord.

KEEP VIGILANT

Simply, without wisdom and understanding, you cannot be vigilant.

"Then he taught me, and he said to me, 'Take hold of My WORDS with ALL your HEART; keep My COMMANDS, and you will live.

Get WISDOM, get UNDERSTANDING; do not forget My words or turn away from them. Do NOT FORSAKE WISDOM, and SHE will PROTECT YOU; love her, and she will watch over you.

The beginning of wisdom is this: get wisdom. Though it COST ALL you have, get UNDERSTANDING.'" (Proverbs 4:4–7)

With wisdom and understanding, our vigilance is to learn to avoid evil at ALL turns—at ALL costs.

Why?

Because evil LIVES to MAKE US STUMBLE.

"Do not set foot on the path of the wicked or walk in the way of evildoers. Avoid it, do not travel on it; turn from it and go on your way.

For they CANNOT REST, UNTIL they DO EVIL; they are ROBBED of SLEEP till they MAKE SOMEONE STUMBLE.

They eat the bread of wickedness and drink the wine of violence. The way of the wicked is like deep darkness;

[Even] they do not know what makes them stumble." (Proverbs 4:14–17, 19)

THEREFORE

"Above all else, GUARD YOUR HEART, for EVERYTHING YOU do FLOWS from it.

Keep your MOUTH FREE of PERVERSITY; keep corrupt talk far from your lips.

Let your EYES LOOK STRAIGHT AHEAD; fix your gaze directly before you.

GIVE CAREFUL THOUGHT to the PATHS for YOUR FEET and be steadfast in all your ways.

DO NOT TURN to the RIGHT or the LEFT; keep your foot from evil." (Proverbs 4:23–27)

WE BELONG TO THE DAY

"Let us keep WIDE AWAKE [Vigilant, Alert, Watchful, Cautious, and on Guard]

And, LET US be SOBER [Calm, Collected, and Circumspect].

We BELONG to the DAY;

Therefore, let us be sober, and put on the breastplate [corslet] of faith, and love, and for a helmet, the hope of salvation." (1 Thessalonians 5:6, 8)

"Devote yourselves to prayer, KEEPING VIGILANT and ALERT in it with an attitude of thanksgiving; praying at the same time...so that we may speak forth the Mystery of Christ." (Colossians 4:2–3)

Since we belong to the DAY (Light), let the LIGHT of Christ (the Anointing) flow through us, thereby no longer living in the night (darkness).

Stay yielded.

Remember, "We're a vessel to whomever we yield."

CHAPTER TWELVE

NEVER BASED ON WHAT "WE DESERVE"

T HIS WILL BE SHORT and to the point.

WE DESERVE NOTHING

As stated previously, we cannot do anything to be worthy enough or good enough to reach God, let alone stay in His Presence.

"For by Grace you have been saved through faith; and that not of yourselves, it is the GIFT of GOD; NOT as a RESULT of [any] WORKS, so that no one may boast."

And,

"All OUR RIGHTEOUSNESS [our best deeds of rightness and justice] are like FILTHY RAGS or a polluted garment."

UNWORTHY SERVANTS

You need to wrap your head around this—we will ALWAYS be unworthy servants—NO MATTER WHAT.

As stated in Luke 17,

"When YOU have done EVERYTHING that was assigned and commanded you, say, we are UNWORTHY SERVANTS [possessing no merit, for we have not gone beyond our obligation]; We have [merely] DONE what was OUR DUTY to do."

IT WAS, IS, AND NEVER WILL BE, BASED ON US

Not "how good."

Not "how religious."

Or even, "how yielded."

We were.

Are.

Or ever will be.

CHAPTER THIRTEEN

SET THESE FOUNDATIONS IN ORDER BEFORE YOU DO ANYTHING

FIRST, FORGIVENESS

WHY IS FORGIVENESS SO important?

You must forgive to be forgiven.

"And when you Stand praying, if you HOLD ANYTHING AGAINST ANYONE, FORGIVE THEM,

So that your Father in Heaven may forgive you, your sins." (Mark 11:25)

"Let all bitterness and wrath and anger and clamor and slander be put away from you, along with all malice.

Be kind to one another, tender-hearted, FORGIVING EACH OTHER, just as GOD in CHRIST also HAS FORGIVEN YOU." (Ephesians 4:31–32)

UNFORGIVENESS IS SPIRITUAL CANCER

It's a cancer that can and will eat us alive—and eventually destroy us.

Taking a moment to veer on a not so slight tangent, I firmly believe that what is true in the spiritual realm will also manifest itself in the physical. So when we play with or allow spiritual cancers to fester, it may well become the truth in our physical realm.

So listen closely.

Even if you don't want to forgive some people—DO IT ANYWAY.

You don't need to like them. You don't need to be friendly or ever have any type relationship with them (again)—that'll be your choice—but you do need to forgive them for WHATEVER they've done—WHATEVER.

I understand in some cases—maybe many cases—that might be an impossible ask—*believe me, I know.*

Remember my father and the insurance policy? He did me WRONG—VERY WRONG!

When he finally found out I had terminal cancer he could've done something to comfort me—even told me—maybe sought medical help for me—he could've tried something—anything. I can understand he was reeling from losing my mother—his wife, six months prior, and now he was about to lose me. But instead, he said nothing and one week later chose to take out an insurance policy on me.

Two insurance agents came to the house to interview my father and me before being able to approve the policy—they asked many questions. *My father "only" lied on the important ones.* I sat there listening in disgust—but said nothing—trying to figure out my next move.

When finally convinced, they stated to approve the policy I needed to go see my doctor to get a "clean bill of health." At which point my father quickly interjected, asking me to confirm that I did NOT need such—stating that since I was in sports and just had a physical six months prior—I wouldn't need another one—and he'd be glad to get them those results. Since that part was true, I said, "Yes, I just had a physical"—so they agreed that was sufficient and granted the policy.

Anyone who knows about boys' physicals back in the day—understands they were *an extensive* height, weight, blood pressure, and "turn your head and cough"—*nothing burger.*

It's one thing if he'd taken out enough to just bury me—that I would've understood—but instead he took out a *MASSIVE* policy on me—not my brothers, just me. *Enough to Cash In and Retire On.* That just *Sucked Beyond Comprehension!* So you can bet I HATED HIM and had NOTHING in my being that would *EVER* want to forgive him.

But one day, down the road, while talking with the Father—out of the clear blue—He asked me to forgive my father. There was no question on what issue to which He was referring.

I didn't like it.

I didn't want to.

I had NO "warm fuzzy feelings" to forgive my father.

I didn't forgive him because he "deserved it."

I didn't forgive him because he asked for forgiveness.

I didn't forgive him because he regretted or repented for what he'd done.

I didn't forgive him because he said he was sorry—in any way—EVER.

111

Which he never admitted to or addressed directly any way—from the inception of the act up to and through his passing twenty plus years later.

It actually had NOTHING to do with him.

I did it to *OBEY* Papa God who I knew loved me no matter what—and when I did a great calm and release came over me in that moment. As I obeyed the Lord, I was able to totally let go of all the hate and anger at the same time—I was free from all of it.

After that my father and I actually became good friends throughout all his remaining years—treating each other on the same level and with respect even though he was forty-six years my senior—talking mostly about engineering since both of us were engineers in our own respective fields.

It was actually funny, that once in a while throughout the years he'd ask out of the clear blue, "Don't you go to one those churches that believe in healing?" I'd simply answer, "Yes, I do." Then he'd stare at me with a puzzled look—waiting—wanting me to elaborate and tell him what he wanted to hear. But being *very stubborn*—hard for you to believe I'm sure—I was determined he'd actually need to break down and ask me directly if he wanted to know what had happened. I felt I was owed that much for all he'd put me through.

Funny thing, guess who canceled the insurance policy three years later?

There's more to this story but this is not the time or venue.

I will mention this to his credit. For a man who NEVER apologized for anything in his life, in his final years he started writing poetry—which did not fit his gruff, left-brained personality—nor had he EVER done so before. He asked me to read it. It was poetry that showed his remorse about *undefined failures* in life. After his passing, I was able to accept that was the very best he could do to apologize to me for everything.

So here's the secret—FORGIVE THE PERSON—not the act (or evil) they did against you. You don't need to accept or forgive their actions—just the person.

In Luke 23:34 as Jesus hung on the cross He said,

"Father, forgive them, for they do not know what they are doing."

Jesus had been beaten, violated, and nailed to a cross, yet He clearly understood that the people were just carrying out the actions taught to them from birth by their father, the ruler of this world.

He forgave the people—not their actions.

Now to take another tangent on top of my current tangent. Oh wow—another double tangent—are you worried that I will be able to circle all the way back? Oh, the humor!

The Lord also wanted me to forgive myself—for blaming me for my mother's cancer—for cussing Him out—and for a MILLION other things.

Have you ever been there—needing to forgive yourself? Many—if not most—if not all have been there at one time or another. If you're like most of us—you don't want to—because you KNOW you do NOT deserve it.

But again, out of OBEDIENCE I did—and again, great calm and release came into my life—immediately—and the guilt and shame never "haunted" me again.

Maybe one of my next books should be called *The Lord is My Therapist* or something similar—if that name isn't taken already. What do you think?

Ok, now I'm back—doubled back!

I understand that we're all a work in progress for as long as we're on this earth. Therefore, I recognize that this subject may be a work in progress as well and difficult for those struggling to forgive.

Sometimes, at best, it's a f—ed up mixed bag in us.

But for me, illuminated by the light that I nearly died of cancer, it made me view forgiveness differently. My eyes were opened. When I finally understood that unforgiveness is spiritual cancer, I learned to detest it—with a passion.

This should be another game of "hot potato" that we learn to throw away as fast as we can.

Nowadays, when somebody does me wrong, I don't hesitate. I throw that unforgiveness away as fast as I can, no matter what they did. As I said, I don't have to like them. I don't need to be a friend to them ever again. That's my choice.

But no matter what, we need to rid ourselves of unforgiveness, ASAP.

Do it for yourself, if no one else. *This is one time that it's totally "OKAY" to be selfish.* Do it for your own health.

Also, in terms of spiritual warfare, if we don't forgive, then we won't be under God's Authority—thereby, we won't be able to have Authority to Stand against evil.

So get rid of it quick.

NEXT, BLESS AND CURSE NOT

We must learn to bless and curse not.

From God's perspective, it's just as important as forgiveness.

Let's take a look at how God views the matter.

"For those the LORD BLESSES, will INHERIT the LAND, but those HE CURSES, will be DESTROYED." (Psalm 37:22)

Along with,

"I will BLESS those, who BLESS YOU, and whoever CURSES YOU, I will CURSE." (Genesis 12:3)

And,

"No one can tame the tongue; it is a restless evil, and full of deadly poison.

With it, we BLESS OUR LORD and Father, and with it, we CURSE MEN, who have been made in the likeness of God;

From the SAME MOUTH come both BLESSING and CURSING.

My brethren, these things ought not to be this way." (James 3:8–10)

We are to,

"Love your enemies, do good to those who hate you,

BLESS those who CURSE YOU,

And pray for those who mistreat you." (Luke 6:27–28)

By cursing, we open up ourselves to the enemy, yielding to him instead of allowing God's Oil (Anointing) to flow through us. Therefore as Golden Pipes, we're channeling, allowing evil to flow through us.

When we curse or even choose not to bless, we're giving (FULL) permission for the wrong spirits to flow through us, becoming channels that empower evil to strike out, creating havoc, destruction, and sometimes death.

Always remember: "We're a vessel to whomever we yield."

WORK OF THE SOUL

This is an aspect of cursing that Dick and I coined as "the work of the soul," "curse-links," and "soul-ties." When we agree with evil, we become a vessel, a channel for evil to spew out of us, directed at whomever we're cursing.

Have you ever "all of a sudden" felt attacked? Fear, depression, oppression, anger and wrath, mentally sick, physically sick, or other ill feelings—all seemingly coming "out of nowhere"? In this case, it may very well be a spiritual issue, not a physical or psychological one.

Maybe you never realized or thought of it in this way. It may be someone purposefully or ignorantly channeling curses and/or evil via the work of their soul.

It might be easier for you to assimilate this when you think of people given over to invoking spells and incantations, such as via witchcraft, but don't be fooled. The ruler of this world has been training EVERYONE on earth from day one—whether they be witches, Christians, non-Christians, and everyday regular people—ALL to be his vessels.

"BLESSED is HE WHO BLESSES YOU [who prays for and contributes to your welfare]

And CURSED is HE WHO CURSES YOU [who in word, thought, or deed would bring harm upon you]." (Numbers 24:9)

"Bless those who persecute you; BLESS and DO NOT CURSE them." (Romans 12:14)

And,

"For I know that he whom You BLESS, is BLESSED, and he whom You CURSE, is CURSED." (Numbers 22:6)

So unless we give ourselves over to God to be His vessels, we, by default, become Satan's vessels.

There's no other choice.

There's no being neutral, no middle ground.

We're either one or the other.

Go back to what we discussed previously—how the enemy wants to deceive us and use us as he controls the earth. The work of the soul is one of his biggest traps—that everyone, including many Christians, easily fall into.

Oops! Did I say Christians again?

Yup! Sure did.

Christians can "pray" evil upon you in the name of "righteousness." Of course, that's BS. It's only them channeling evil by the work of the soul.

Sad, but true.

The enemy has planned this from his fall. He knows that unless we are yielded to God, he wins big time, allowing a highway of hell to be unleashed over and over and over again.

We will expand on the work of the soul as well as simple solutions to handle such later.

JUDGEMENT

Judgment that we talked about previously—God's white throne character judgment, the type that we're NOT supposed to do—is similar to and in the same basket as cursing.

Let's take another moment to veer onto the same tangent discussed previously.

This kind of judgment, along with unforgiveness (as cancer) and cursing, are issues of the heart (or the land). Once again, I firmly believe that what is true in the spiritual realm will also manifest itself in the physical, so when we play with or allow negative spiritual heart or land issues, it may well become the truth in our physical realm.

HERE'S A TOUGH ONE

How do we bless people when we believe (know) they've done us or others wrong?

First, remember God said,

"I will BLESS those, WHO BLESS YOU, and WHOEVER CURSES YOU, I will CURSE."

That's His job, not ours. Vengeance is the Lord's.

Second, we may be tempted to pray, "God get them," "God stop them," "God teach them," or similar rhetoric.

These words are borderline curses, if not straight up curses—the opposite of blessings. The only difference may be intent, but how can we really be sure that our intent is good?

If we're hurt, if we're pissed, if we think we're in the right and they're wrong, if we think we're righteous or spiritual, our intent is probably not good. God knows our heart. Don't fool yourself. You're not fooling Him.

We're to pray against evil, not people, no matter what they did to us, no matter how we cloak our prayers in "religiosity," "spirituality," or "our (perceived) righteousness."

SO HOW SHOULD WE PRAY?

What if I told you there are two secrets to God's BLESSINGs?

The *first secret* is envisioning a regular plain 'ol blessing from God's perspective.

When we think of "blessings," we envision that were supposed to pray for "rainbows," "roses," and "unicorns"—all "fluffy," "puffy," and "wrapped in a warm blanket."

God's perspective is different.

His blessings are meant to do WHATEVER it takes to bring people to Himself. That isn't always nice.

How did God treat Moses when he didn't obey? How did he treat Job who did obey? How did he treat Israel—over and over again—to redirect them onto His path?

Any "rainbows," "roses," "unicorns," "fluffy," "puffy," and "wrapped in warm blankets" there? That would be a big N— O—.

Were those God's blessings?

YES.

His intent is perfect.

If that's the blessings He did for His own people, how much more do you think He'll do to others?

We must learn how to use His intent to pray blessings without cursing.

Now building on His WHATEVERS—the *second secret* is to understand what the word "blessing" actually means to God.

Remembering what Genesis 12:3 and other scriptures, above, said about God?

"I will BLESS those, WHO BLESS YOU, and WHOEVER CURSES YOU, I will CURSE."

The words *Bless* and *Blessed* in the Hebrew are 'barak' (baw-rak), a prim root which ENCOMPASSES not only "bless," "abundantly bless," "actually blessed," "bless is blessed," "bless me indeed," "bless them at all," "blessed," "blessed be those who bless," "blessed is everyone who blesses," "blesses," "blessing," but also ENCOMPASSES, "curse," "cursed," and "curses."

Oops!

Did I mean what I just said—that the same word for blessings is the same word for curses?

YUP.

How do we reconcile that?

When do we know which interpretation of the word "barak" to use?

Good News!

We don't need to know—EVER.

Because God is God—and as God, He will choose when *Blessings* are meant to be "blessings" and when *Blessings* are meant to be "curses."

Therefore when we pray "blessings," without cursing, God is in charge of the WHATEVERS.

Let's learn a new language and intent—no longer "God get them," "God stop them," or "God teach them."

How about? "God, stop the evil behind, surrounding, or influencing them" (later we'll discuss how to use the Authority given us to do that in our Stand) and "Do WHATEVER it takes to bring them to you," remembering what "WHATEVER" means to God.

It means—*WHATEVER.*

When we pray that way, it ALWAYS leaves it up to God to do WHATEVER it takes—not our feelings, intent, or judgement. We can rest assured that God's blessings will be all the "roses" or "thorns" needed to bring them to His good end. When we get a hold of His perceptions and understandings, we can rest assured in His blessing.

Lord, teach us how to pray Your way, praying against all the evil that's behind the people, not against the people themselves, praying the people can come to know You when evil is removed from the equation.

In terms of spiritual warfare, if we CURSE and DON'T BLESS, we WON'T be UNDER GOD'S AUTHORITY nor be able to successfully Stand against evil—instead, evil will get away with "murder."

A little sidenote: Am I saying that all cancers and/or heart issues are caused by spiritual negligence?

Absolutely NOT.

But are some?

YES.

We all screw up, so let's not get caught up in our failures. Instead, it's up to each one of us to be diligent to not allow any of these spiritual issues to remain long enough that they become physical ones.

NEXT, REPENTING OF OUR SINS

"The acts of the flesh are obvious: sexual immorality, impurity and debauchery; idolatry and witchcraft; hatred, discord, jealousy, fits of rage, selfish ambition, dissensions, factions and envy; drunkenness, orgies, and the like." (Galatians 5:19–21)

Once again, before we get down on ourselves or one another, let's agree we all screw up. We have the option to waste our life wallowing in our failures, but let's not. It's not about being perfect.

Let's live, learn, clean up the poop, and move on.

It's really about yielding, repenting, and asking the Lord to help us.

Why is this important since we've been saved by Grace and already received forgiveness?

Three reasons:

First, what we choose here and now, we will get for eternity—whether you understand it or not—the earth is a testing ground. This is the basis and difference between the Kingdoms—the Kingdom of Heaven and the Kingdom of God—which we will not take the time to discuss here—that'll take another book.

Second, there are the obvious health issues that sin can bring—spiritual, physical, psychological, mental, emotional, and other.

Third, simply again, because we cannot expect to operate with Authority. When we yield to sin and evil, we're not under Authority.

SO, WHAT'S THE OPPOSITE OF THE ABOVE?

To live by the fruit of the Spirit (the ANOINTING) and to walk in the Spirit (the ANOINTING).

"The fruit of the Spirit [the ANOINTING] is love, joy, peace, forbearance, kindness, goodness, faithfulness, gentleness and self-control. Against such things there is no law.

Those who belong to CHRIST [the ANOINTING] Jesus have crucified the flesh with its passions and desires.

Since we live by the Spirit [the ANOINTING], let us also walk in the Spirit [the ANOINTING]." (Galatians 5:22–25)

IN CONCLUSION

Again, "Let us not become boastful and self-conceited, competitive and challenging and provoking and irritating to one another, envying and being jealous of one another."

As well as,

"Therefore, be imitators of God, as beloved children; and walk in love, just as Christ [the ANOINTING] also loved you and gave Himself up for us, an offering and a sacrifice to God as a fragrant aroma. But immorality or any impurity or greed must not even be named among you, as is proper among saints; and there must be no filthiness and silly talk, or coarse jesting, which are not fitting, but rather giving of thanks.

For this you know with certainty, that no immoral or impure person or covetous man, who is an idolater, has an inheritance in the Kingdom of Christ and God.

Let no one deceive you with empty words, for because of these things the wrath of God comes upon the sons of disobedience. Therefore, do not be partakers with them; for you were formerly darkness, but now you are Light in the Lord; walk as children of Light (for the fruit of the Light consists in all goodness and righteousness and Truth), trying to learn what is pleasing to the Lord.

Do not participate in the unfruitful deeds of darkness, but instead even expose them; for it is disgraceful even to speak of the things which are done by them in secret. But all things become visible when they are exposed by the light, for everything that becomes visible is light. For this reason it says, 'Awake, sleeper, and arise from the dead, and Christ [the ANOINTING] will shine on you.'

Therefore, be careful how you walk, not as unwise men but as wise, making the most of your time, because the days are evil. So then do not be foolish, but understand what the will of the Lord is. And do not get drunk with wine, for that is dissipation, but be filled with the Spirit [the ANOINTING], speaking to one another in psalms and hymns and spiritual songs, singing and making melody with your heart to the Lord;

always giving thanks for all things in the name of our Lord Jesus Christ to God, even the Father;" (Ephesians 5:1-20)

CHAPTER FOURTEEN

KEYS

W HAT ARE SOME OF the keys we must have in place to be able to operate under God's Authority?

Let's review some of the things we've talked about to this point.

THE ANOINTING

We must be In CHRIST for His Anointing to flow through us, enabling rivers of living waters to flow from our innermost being, which will then overflow throughout our lives and beyond.

Without the Anointing, we're just operating on our own power, in the flesh, no Authority.

Walking in the Anointing enables God's Authority.

YIELDING

We can only receive the Anointing, the infilling of Christ, by yielding ourselves to the Lord.

As discussed, we're nothing more than pipes, conduits, vessels, and channels for the spirit world. Either we become those vessels for the Holy Spirit or for evil to flow—our choice—knowingly or not—no other option.

Yielding to the Lord enables God's Authority.

HUMILITY

Without it, we have nothing.

Submission won't work.

Resisting won't work.

Fleeing won't happen.

A simple formula for failure—NO humility equals NO submission equals NO resisting equals NO enemy fleeing.

A simple formula for success—humility PLUS submission PLUS resisting equals the enemy fleeing.

Humility enables God's Authority.

FORGIVENESS

Unforgiveness is a spiritual cancer that can eat us up from the inside out.

Unforgiveness disables God's Authority from flowing through us.

To the converse, *forgiveness enables God's Authority to flow.*

BLESSING, NOT CURSING

Once again, cursing is a spiritual heart condition that can destroy us from the inside out.

Cursing can disable us from operating in God's Authority *while blessing enables God's Authority.*

Remember how God blesses, and it's His job to decide and do the WHATEVERs.

NO (WHITE THRONE) JUDGEMENTS

Whereas all levels of discernment and judging right from wrong for ourselves and others is fine. To the opposite, acting as a judge, condemning, passing judgment as God judges, invoking white throne judgement on people's characters is another spiritual condition that can disable us from God's Authority, as well as, eventually severely harm or destroy us.

Removing (white throne) judgements from our midst enables God's Authority.

LOVE

Sounds obvious.

There are numerous words in the Greek for *love*, but we're told to love others with God's love, "Agape."

AGAPE is God's unconditional love toward us—in spite of us.

In First Corinthians 13:1–13, we're told,

"If I speak in the tongues of men or of angels, but do not have [AGAPE], I am only a resounding gong or a clanging cymbal.

If I have the gift of prophecy and can fathom all mysteries and all knowledge, and if I have a faith that can move mountains, but do not have [AGAPE], I am nothing.

If I give all I possess to the poor and give over my body to hardship that I may boast, but do not have [AGAPE], I gain nothing...

[AGAPE] is patient, [AGAPE] is kind. It does not envy, it does not boast, it is not proud. It does not dishonor others, it is not self-seeking, it is not easily angered, it keeps no record of wrongs.

[AGAPE] does not delight in evil but rejoices with the Truth. It always protects, always trusts, always hopes, always perseveres.

[AGAPE] never fails...

And now these three remain: faith, hope and [AGAPE]. But the greatest of these is [AGAPE]."

AGAPE enables God's Authority.

PRAYER

This also should be obvious.

We are to,

"Be unceasing in prayer [praying perseveringly]." (1 Thessalonians 5:17)

Simply put, prayer is talking to God.

No rules, no rote, no religious forms, etc.

As the (trademarked by Nike) saying goes, "Just do it."

Remember the warnings. Always pray against evil, not people.

Conversely, you can ALWAYS pray blessings for and over people.

This kind of prayer enables God's Authority.

UNDER GOD'S AUTHORITY

As discussed in numerous ways to this point, *we must be Under God's Authority to have Authority.* Not our authority—not men's or women's authority—*God's Authority.*

Without it, we will get the crap beat out of us like the Seven Sons of Sceva. See the next chapter for details.

PEACE OF GOD

"And the Peace of God, which surpasses all understanding [comprehension], will guard your hearts and your minds in Christ Jesus." (Philippians 4:7)

We need to learn to operate in and live by the Peace that passes understanding.

We can clearly know what is from God because of HIS PEACE—not "a peace."

When we stop and yield our hearts to the Father, He will give us His Peace in the best and worst of times.

So when thoughts come, how do we distinguish which is God's still small voice versus the enemy's tangents and deceptions (coming via the power of the air)?

Simply by HIS PEACE that PASSES UNDERSTANDING.

This is how we can differentiate God's direction verses the enemy's.

We can learn how to tell them apart by knowing God's Word then sensing if God's Peace that passes understanding is there or not. Remember, the enemy knows God's Word better than us, so the Word by itself is not enough.

WARNING ABOUT "A PEACE"

"A peace" is NOT "THE PEACE."

"THE PEACE" is God's Peace that passes understanding.

Growing up in the church, many would say, "I was praying, and I got a peace." Not good enough.

We can get "a peace" when we just ate a good meal and our bellies are full.

We can get "a peace" when we calm ourselves down.

We can get "a peace" when we stop and pray.

We can get "a peace" when we meditate.

We can get "a peace" when the enemy wants to deceive us.

"A peace" does NOT pass understanding.

"A peace" does NOT surround us with His Anointing.

In the upcoming "FASTING IS WARFARE" chapter, I share a great example—a believer who, after fasting and praying, said she got "a peace." See how that worked out for her.

AND, AGAIN, BEWARE OF THE THINGS THAT WILL TAKE US DOWN

PRIDE

Our ego will always destroy us.

Be sure that the ruler of this earth is always prowling around, looking for ways to destroy us.

Pride and ego are big ones—he knows them well because they are why he fell from Heaven.

In Proverbs 16:18–19, we're told,

"Pride goes before destruction, and a haughty spirit before stumbling.

It is better to be humble in spirit with the lowly than to divide the spoil with the proud."

This kind of *pride* in the Hebrew is 'gaon' (ga-own), whose meaning includes "exaltation," "arrogance," "eminence," (thinking you're) "majestic," (thinking you deserve) "pomp," and surprisingly includes "thickets" (like things you could get stuck in when out in the forest or fields).

This is the same type pride that Lucifer had towards God. Lucifer fell under the false puffed-up belief that he was greater than God, his creator, thereby causing his removal from Heaven.

LUST FOR POWER AND CONTROL

Such desires, whether in the church or the world, will make us ineffective for God, His Church, and the world.

They are tools for the enemy to destroy us.

THE MISUSE OF SEXUAL DESIRES

Sex is great.

Beyond procreation—it's meant to be a great pleasure—when used as God intended—but be sure that the enemy will try to distort a good thing for evil.

It has been a source of failure for many.

So be careful.

LOVING OR WORSHIPING MONEY

Money can be an effective tool, but that is much different from loving or worshiping it (1 Timothy 6:10)—more on that later.

FIND THE BALANCE

As Dick used to say to me back in the early days. "My head was so far up in the clouds that I was no earthly good."

Unfortunately, he was right.

That was true for a long time, but God "graciously" changed me—and I say that with all facetiousness.

As I mentioned previously, keep your eyes and hearts in the clouds, but keep your mind and feet firmly planted on the earth.

THEN YOU CAN STAND

CHAPTER FIFTEEN

WARNING: THE SEVEN SONS OF SCEVA

OPERATE WITH REAL AUTHORITY OR DON'T DO IT AT ALL

I F YOU DON'T, YOU'LL get your ass kicked.

JUST LIKE THE SEVEN SONS OF SCEVA

In Acts 19:13–16, we see where there were,

"Some of the Jewish exorcists, who went from place to place, attempting to name over those who had evil spirits the name of the Lord Jesus,

Saying, 'In the name of the Jesus whom Paul preaches, I command you to come out.'

Seven Sons of one Sceva, a Jewish chief priest, were doing this.

And, the evil spirit answered, and said to them,

'Jesus, I know, and I know about Paul, but who [in the hell] are you?'

And the man, in whom was the evil spirit, leaped on them, and subdued all of them, and overpowered them, so that they fled out of that house naked and wounded."

Dealing with the enemy is NOT a game!

Let me repeat myself,

Dealing with the enemy is NOT a game!

Remember that the devil is fifty-foot-tall compared to us.

He's the most powerful being God ever made.

He's the ruler of this world.

If you treat him with any less respect, you're a fool.

We can NEVER defeat him on our own.

If we try, we will get our asses handed to us like the seven sons.

DICK

I'm reminded of a time about Dick.

Dick was an elder and assistant pastor. During the days, though, the job he had that paid the bills was as a science teacher and coach. He'd been doing that at a local junior high school for many years.

The school's mascot and name for all their sports teams was the "Blue Devils." Every day he'd walk into school, look at the large painting of an animated blue devil in the hallway and cringe.

One day, as he was giving me a tour of his workplace, he'd had enough. He looked at that painting on the wall as we passed by and announced, "Devil, I take you on. You will not rule here any longer."

Almost sounds good, right?

Well, it wasn't.

By the end of the day, a man who was never sick became violently ill.

He went home that day and remained that way for almost a week—until he realized the error of his ways.

He finally comprehended that he had confronted the devil out of his own ego and power.

Therefore, the devil loved the opportunity to beat the $hit out of him.

Dick was used to seeing God's Power over and over in spiritual warfare—but he forgot.

It had always been the Lord giving him the Authority, via God's faith in the moment, that was operating through him, never himself.

When his eyes were opened, he repented, and IMMEDIATELY he was well again.

He learned a big lesson—so should we.

YIELDED BELIEVER

Being willing to repeat myself over and over and over again—you must be a yielded believer.

Never play around with Authority—EVER.

I like guns—as long as they're used with all safety—but playing with Authority is like giving a child a loaded gun then wondering why someone got hurt or killed.

AS A YIELDED BELIEVER, THE ANOINTING AND GOD'S AUTHORITY WILL FLOW THROUGH YOU IN ALL YOU DO

FISHING

There was another time when two ladies from our homegroup asked if I could take them fishing.

I was an avid outdoorsman and love fishing.

So one evening, I took them to a favorite spot on a river where the white bass had been running. Even though it was called a river, at this part it was only a large creek, about thirty feet across and maybe a couple of feet deep.

We parked the car a few hundred yards away then walked down to the river with our gear.

Normally, when the run was in full steam, you'd be forced to stand shoulder-to-shoulder with others. Unfortunately, the run was over, and no one was there but us.

Determined to make the best of the situation, hoping there might still be a few white bass in the stream, as determined fishermen we stayed.

We found a good spot and stood on the same side, with about twenty feet between each of us—the ladies on the left and me on the right—giving each other plenty enough room for casting our lures without entangling each other's line.

As we stood there fishing—actually just casting, not catching a thing—two men walked up from around the bend, wading in the middle of the river.

I'm not a small guy—I was five feet eight inches and probably around 285 pounds at the time—but these guys were much bigger. They dwarfed me. They had to be six feet four inches to six feet six inches and 350 to 400 pounds each. You could tell that they were thicker and more muscular than fat.

The men came around the bend to my right, maybe thirty feet away. I got an extremely uneasy feeling, but trying to be cordial, I said, "How's it going?"

One of the men grumbled an unfriendly, unintelligible reply.

The uneasy feeling continued to get much worse, so in my mind, under my breath, I bound and cut off all the enemy.

They stood there and did not move for five long, long minutes, then they walked over next to each other and began whispering in each other's ears, scanning back and forth at the two ladies and me.

At that point, they walked right in front of where we were fishing, forcing us to change where we were casting. We tried to be nice, ignoring their disrespect.

For another long five minutes, they continued to look back and forth at us and then each other.

The uneasy feeling became ominous.

The atmosphere was "so thick you could cut it with a knife."

There were overwhelming feelings of rape and murder.

The women and I glanced back and forth at each other, our faces expressing grave concern as if we all knew what was about to happen.

It felt unquestionably hopeless as if we tried to leave or run, they'd chase us down, kill me, and have their way with the women, then kill them.

Then when it felt like all was about to climax, I very discretely felt for my hunting knife at my side.

I knew that I'd die before letting them get to the women. I'd do whatever it took to give the women a chance to run back to the car.

I felt like it was going to be my end because each one outclassed me physically. My only solace was, as I fought to the end, that the women could get up the bank, back to the car, and get away.

Now the time became imminent.

So for a second time, in my mind and under my breath, I again began to bind and cut off all the enemy.

INSTANTLY!

Before I could even finish my thoughts, one of the men screamed out at the top of his lungs!

"SHUT UP!"

"WE HEARD YOU THE FIRST TIME!"

"WE'RE LEAVING!"

At which point, they immediately turned tail and quickly rounded the bend of the river from where they had come until gone and out of sight.

For some long moments, I stood there in shock.

So did the women.

A couple of minutes later, the ladies came over.

They expressed that they had felt the exact same thick overwhelming atmosphere of rape and murder. They, too, had felt the same pending feelings of doom.

Flabbergasted, they asked, "What did you say that made them yell that crazy stuff and made them leave?"

I repeated, "I only said, 'How's it going?' some fifteen minutes earlier."

They acknowledged they'd heard that but still wondered what had just happened in front of them.

I told them that the only other thing I'd done in the beginning—in my mind, under my breath—I'd *bound the enemy.*

Then as things came to a head and for a second time, I once again, in my mind, under my breath, *bound the enemy.*

That's when the man said what he said, and they left.

We all stood there stunned, amazed, shocked.

As the adrenaline began to drain from my body, I stood there shaking.

The only thing flowing through my mind was the scripture,

"Greater is He who is in you than he who is in the world." (1 John 4:4)

We saw it firsthand.

The Holy Spirit, who's in us, is greater than all the evil spirits in all others; and, boy, am I glad He is!

CHAPTER SIXTEEN

FASTING IS WARFARE

SPIRITUAL FASTING

H ERE I'M TALKING ABOUT spiritual fasting, not physical fasting for diet or health reasons.

Many people make the mistake believing that fasting is to get closer to God—specifically to hear from Him about their concerns and get answers.

Unfortunately, that's NOT correct.

Fasting is warfare.

Remember yielding?

To whomever you yield, you become a vessel, a channel for them to flow through.

Well, fasting is YIELDING on STEROIDS.

It's meant to be yielding that allows the Holy Spirit to flow through us, to fight spiritual battles for ourselves and the people for whom we're praying.

IT'S FRONTLINE BATTLING THE ENEMY

When you're on the front lines, facing the enemy, weapons in hand, swinging your sword, it is NOT the time to be looking backward and having a nice "chitchat," talking to the Father to get "answers."

Don't get me wrong.

After the fast and the battle, you may get answers from God because you just fought for them—just not during the fight.

Jesus fasted for forty days. Did he talk to the Father during that time? Did he use it to get great revelations or answers to prayer?

NO.

It was a time to test Him.

He was doing battle.

In the end, the devil tempted Him, but Jesus stood firm against him and defeated him.

An example of warfare is shown in Matthew 17:19–21, where,

"The disciples came to Jesus and said, 'Why could we not drive the demon out?'

Jesus answered, 'THIS KIND does NOT go out EXCEPT by PRAYER and FASTING.'"

LET'S LOOK AT HOW THE ENEMY USES FASTING WITH THE UNINFORMED

Many good-hearted people are taught and believe if they fast, they can get close to God and hear from Him.

Unfortunately, *they will be deceived.*

They'll think they're hearing from God, but instead, it's the enemy; for the many doing this lack knowledge, and the devil will take advantage of their ignorance to attempt to send them down the wrong path.

They're on the frontlines, facing the enemy, who knows he's there to do battle with them, but they think they're there to have a "chitchat" with God.

Don't you think that the deceiver *will laugh* as he takes advantage of that situation to give them "answers" from *god* (he, with the little "g")?

A good example was with a woman—a born-again believer—who was unhappy with her life.

As a good Christian, she decided to fast and pray. She wanted to hear from God to get direction for her life, to find happiness again.

During her fast, she said she "heard from God" and God told her to become a Mormon, so she gave up her marriage, her family, her life, moved to Salt Lake City, and did just that.

Afterward, she no longer had any big troubles in her life. She said she now had "a peace." She was "happy." Therefore, that convinced her she had heard right.

Don't get me wrong.

She did hear from *god*—once again with a little "g"—the *god* of this world.

What do you think?

Don't you know that if you give yourself over to any tangent offered from the ruler of this world, he won't let up on the troubles he's been sending?

He doesn't care how he wins.

As long as if he can win, he can make you ineffective for God.

CHAPTER SEVENTEEN

THE FORMULA AND "MAGIC" PRAYERS

ARE YOU LOOKING FOR THE FORMULA AND/OR "MAGIC" PRAYERS?

T HAT'S BS.

We're not going to say the Lord's Prayer here—and nothing against some wonderful Catholic believers that have met and love the Lord—but we're not going to play, repeating the rosary or some other rote prayer, over and over, believing it has power.

And even if I could tell you some "magic" set of prayers—I wouldn't—because it would just become rote over time.

You'd just be repeating what I said with no Power or Authority behind you.

You'd end up getting your ass kicked—exactly like the Seven Sons of Sceva.

So if that's what you're looking for you're in the wrong place and I'm not going to give them to you.

So make a choice, then move on. Either get back to learning this manual, step-by-step, or find some teachings elsewhere that will fancy the facades you'd rather believe in.

THE POWER OF PRAYER

Without concern of repeating myself, this should be obvious. We are to,

"Be unceasing in prayer (praying perseveringly)."

Simply put, prayer is talking to God.

No rules, no rote, no religious forms, etc.

As stated, "Just do it."

The only set of guardrails is to pray within God's will and by His (generated) faith.

NO GOSSIPING

Let's take a moment to fix a BIG problem in the church.

Prayer is not an excuse to gossip.

You say, "WHAT?"

Yes, I mean gossip.

Some of the worst gossipers are in the church.

It used to be that we envisioned gossipers to be two little old ladies standing on either side of the fence, whispering all the neighborhood chatter to each other, saying, "Did you hear about this", "that", or "so and so?" Giggling, gasping.

Nowadays, it's become the norm for believers in churches.

They start with a "pray request."

"Oh, who's it for?"

"What's it about?"

Then repeating it, "Did you hear about this", "that", or "so and so?"

Still gasping, maybe not giggling (at least publicly).

Gosh, that wouldn't be very Christian of them, would it?

Living to get the dirty details so they can repeat "passing (every bit of) it along" to all the prayer trees, prayer chains, prayer request lines, etc.

This is BS.

It must stop!

If you have a prayer request, it should be told with as MINIMAL information as is necessary.

It should NEVER be expanded upon, no matter how much others want to know or ask.

Simply, "Pray for Sally, she's going through a difficult time" or "Pray for Ron and his family for health issues."

No gossip, no details, no elaboration, no filling in the blanks, no answering anyone's questions about them.

Do you really believe the Father needs to hear the nitty-gritty (gossiping) details from us, so then—and only then—He finally knows how to help them?

Wow!

How did He ever get along before all the gossips got involved?

Nowadays, when I receive a "prayer tree" email or any kind of notification, I no longer open it. All I do is stop, cut off all the evil and such behind or coming against the people, things, or situations (that have been noted inside the request(s))—then take the time to pray in the Spirit according to all you'll learn in this manual—listening to the Holy Spirit for each—praying in agreement with ALL that the Spirit would have praying in that moment.

Why?

If the Father doesn't know who they are and how to help them, then we're all sunk!

CHAPTER EIGHTEEN

THE ARMOR OF GOD

AFTER YOU HAVE DONE EVERYTHING TO STAND FIRM, STAND FIRM

"FINALLY, BE STRONG IN the Lord and in His mighty Power. Put on the full armor of God, so that you can take your STAND against the devil's schemes.

For our struggle is not against flesh and blood, but against the rulers, against the authorities, against the powers of this dark world and against the spiritual forces of evil in the heavenly realms.

Therefore, put on the full armor of God, so that when the day of evil comes, you may be able to STAND your ground,

And, AFTER you have done EVERYTHING to STAND firm, STAND firm

Therefore, having girded your loins with (the belt of) Truth,

And having put on the breastplate of righteousness,

And having shod your feet with the preparation of the gospel of Peace;

In addition to all, taking up the shield of faith with which you will be able to extinguish ALL the flaming arrows of the evil one.

And take the helmet of salvation,

And the sword of the Spirit, which is the Word of God." (Ephesians 6:10–14)

This subject is taught often, so we won't spend a lot of time reviewing it, but I will put my tweak on it in light of things we've covered to this point.

FIRST, PUT ON TRUTH

God is the God of Truth.

We're told to gird our loins with the belt of Truth.

What type of belt is God talking about?

A chastity belt.

A chastity belt protects, covers the loins and our private parts. Why does God say that here? Because if we don't have God's Truth protecting our (spiritual) private parts, we'll end up having (spiritual) intercourse with the wrong things.

That intercourse can be with many things in or of this world where we fall for the enemy's enticements or tricks.

You cannot defeat an enemy that you're "sleeping with."

So, be real.

Be honest.

Love the Truth.

SECOND, PUT ON YOUR SHOES

It says to shod your feet with the preparation of the gospel of Peace.

Many think and teach that we're to put the gospel of Peace on our feet—but that's wrong—that's not what it says—it says the preparation.

What's the preparation?

Repentance.

You can't receive the gospel unless you repent, at which point, we can have The Peace that passes understanding, guiding our feet as we walk into battle.

We've discussed the importance of repentance and The Peace earlier.

THIRD, TAKE UP THE SHIELD OF FAITH

Faith is the only shield that can extinguish all the flaming arrows of the enemy—God's faith in God's will, operating by God's direction.

As discussed earlier, when we're under God's Authority, the faith that He gives us is different—180 degrees different.

He doesn't want our faith. He doesn't want garbage faith. He doesn't want any kind of faith we can "muster up."

He doesn't want the "faithers" faith, who magically believe that if they try hard enough, they can proclaim "whatever" into being. I guess they believe in rubbing the "genie in the bottle," but again, I digress.

FORTH, PUT ON THE HELMET OF SALVATION

Without question, we cannot do anything without God's salvation through Jesus.

We must recognize that salvation is FULLY COMPLETE.

It was COMPLETED at the CROSS.

I know there are many who spend a lot of time arguing the difference in scriptures—ones that say "was saved," "being saved," or "will be saved"—ones that mention "justification," "sanctification," or "glorification"—some who argue once saved, always saved versus those who say you can lose your salvation and must earn it back every day.

Many wasting their time arguing such are not dealing with salvation correctly. They need to see it in the light of the body, the soul, and the spirit as seen in the Word.

No matter the opinions—salvation was COMPLETED at the CROSS—so put it on.

That helmet will protect your mind and thoughts.

FIFTH, PICK UP THE SWORD OF THE SPIRIT

Which is the Word of God.

We typically call the Bible "the Word," and it is.

But the LIVING "Word (CHRIST) became flesh, and dwelt among us, and we saw His Glory, Glory as of the only begotten Son from the Father, full of Grace and Truth." (John 1:14)

Yet, once again, we've come full circle, back to Christ, the ANOINTING.

So, yes, while we need to know the Bible, God's Word, we must have the Living Word, the Fullness of God in Christ, in His Spirit, flowing through us.

But even more important, we must YIELD as a funnel, a channel for the ANOINTING to flow—if we're to defeat the enemy.

NOW, IT'S TIME TO STAND

Put on the full armor of God so that when the day of evil comes, "You may be ABLE to STAND."

I love the way it says—and "After you have done EVERYTHING to *STAND*, then *STAND*."

In other words, after you've done everything you can to prepare to STAND, *then just do it!*

CHAPTER NINETEEN

IN THE NAME OF JESUS

WHAT'S THE NAME OF JESUS?

*H*IS NAME IS CHRIST—THE *ANOINTING.*

"At the Name of Jesus, every knee will bow, of those who are in Heaven and on earth and under the earth, and that every tongue will confess that Jesus Christ is Lord." (Philippians 2:10–11)

His Name is not just any ol' name like Tom, Dick, Sally, or Jane. No one and nothing in Heaven or earth will ever bow to any of our names, nor should they.

What's in the Name of Jesus?

Power.

ALL the Power of the Godhead.

ALL the Power that created the earth and everything in it.

ALL the Power that holds everything together by the Word of His mouth.

JESUS IS THE LIGHT, THE TRUTH, AND THE BLOOD

So when we speak in the Name of Jesus, we are speaking forth the Light, the Truth, and the Blood—along with ALL the Power of God.

THE TRUTH

As established, God is the God of Truth.

Grace and Truth came through Jesus Christ (the Anointing).

The Truth will set us free.

The Truth reveals, exposes, and defeats ALL lies.

The Truth defeats ALL evil.

THE BLOOD

The Blood is the completion of the sacrifice by Jesus.

He came to earth as the perfect Son of God, lived, then died for all of us on the cross.

That Blood won ALL.

Heals ALL.

Covers ALL.

Protects ALL.

Defeats ALL.

"And, they OVERCAME him [the accuser of our brethren] BECAUSE of THE BLOOD of THE LAMB, and because of the word of their testimony." (Revelation 12:10)

THE BLOOD IS OUR COVERING

It's a shield that protects us from ALL the evil ARROWS and ANY KIND of WEAPONS sent against us.

"No WEAPON formed against you will prosper.

And every tongue that accuses you in judgment you will condemn.

This is the heritage of the servants of the LORD,

And their vindication is from Me," declares the LORD." (Isaiah 54:17)

"You will not be afraid of the terror by night, or of the ARROW that flies by day." (Psalm 91:5)

It's a dome of protection that reflects ALL ARROWS and ALL WEAPONS (of any type) back to the senders.

"The LORD *shall return their evil on their own head*." (1 Kings 2:44)

THE LIGHT

God spoke Light into being.

God brought His Light to live with and in us through Jesus, His sacrifice, and resurrection.

This is (Son) Light.

It reveals.

It heals.

It exposes.

It destroys.

It dispels darkness—it makes darkness flee at the speed of Light.

Remember the story of Jehoshaphat?

In Second Chronicles 20:15–23, it's recorded how Israel was being attacked by three vast armies.

"Listen, King Jehoshaphat and all who live in Judah and Jerusalem! ... 'Do not be afraid or discouraged because of this vast army.

For the battle is not yours, but God's ... You will not have to fight this battle.

Take up your positions; STAND firm and see the deliverance the Lord will give you.

Do not be afraid; do not be discouraged. Go out to face them tomorrow, and the Lord will be with you.' ...

Jehoshaphat appointed men to sing to the Lord and to praise Him, for the splendor of His holiness, as they went out at the head of the army,

Saying: 'Give thanks to the Lord, for His love endures forever.'

As they began to sing and praise,

The LORD SET AMBUSHES [TRAPS] against the men of Ammon and Moab and Mount Seir who were invading Judah,

And, THEY WERE DEFEATED.

The Ammonites and Moabites rose up against the men from Mount Seir to destroy and annihilate them.

AFTER THEY FINISHED slaughtering the men from Seir, they helped to DESTROY ONE ANOTHER."

In the church, the typical teachings about this event emphasize singing, praise, and worship—all good things—wonderful stuff—but that's not what defeated the vast armies coming against Israel.

Instead, it was the Lord SETTING AMBUSHES [TRAPS] against them.

What kind of traps could make the armies attacking Israel turn and destroy themselves in unison? We're not told exactly, but let's talk LIGHT.

Light can be great, but have you ever been blinded by the sun?

Most of us have, at one point or another, whether driving, cycling, walking, in sports, or other.

Actually, it's NOT fun at all—I HATE driving with the sun in my eyes.

My guess is that God blinded them with blaring overwhelming sunlight from all sides—reflections and views they could not get around—maybe reflecting off every helmet, breastplate, shield, and sword of everyone in all three armies—and who knows if God didn't even make reflections off the water, grass, and rocks. All that, in turn, caused them to go into confusion, attack one another, and destroy one another.

Sunlight is the physical representation of the "Son Light."

When the Light is shined on us, it can light our way—but it can also cause confusion as well as cause darkness to flee at the speed of light—in this case for the enemies of Israel.

JESUS, THE NAME AND POWER OF GOD, INCARNATE

Why do you think that demons cringed in fear whenever Jesus came around?

"In the synagogue there was a man possessed by demon[s], impure spirit[s]; he cried out at the top of his voice,

'Go away! What do you want with us, Jesus of Nazareth? Have you come to destroy us? I know who you are—the Holy One of God!'" (Luke 4:33–34)

Now stop and think. This was the enemy's response before Jesus ascended, so how do you think they perceive Him now?

They cringe in even greater fear and, worse, that the Church might learn to yield to God. Then, by the name of Jesus, eradicate them (destroy them) from within the heavens and earth.

AN ABSOLUTE KEY TO STANDING SUCCESSFULLY

~

WE MUST LEARN AND OPERATE IN THE NAME OF JESUS

The Light.

The Truth.

The Blood.

And, the Word.

CHAPTER TWENTY

BINDING, LOOSING, AND CUTTING OFF

BINDING AND LOOSING

That which is bound on earth, is bound in heaven.

That which is loosed on earth, is loosed in heaven.

Jesus said,

"WHATEVER YOU BIND [forbid and declare to be improper and unlawful] ON EARTH shall have been BOUND [forbidden and declared to be improper and unlawful] IN HEAVEN; And WHATEVER YOU LOOSE [permit and declare to be proper and lawful] ON EARTH shall have been LOOSED [permitted and declared to be proper and lawful] IN HEAVEN." (Matthew 18:18)

So what does that mean for us in STANDING?

In light that we've been given ALL Power over ALL the enemy, it means we have the ability to bind and loose.

Notice, unfortunately, He didn't just limit us to binding up the enemy to stop evil and loosing the Spirit of God for good—which, obviously, is what we should be doing.

Instead, conversely, without limits, we can bind up the work of God (good) and loose the enemy (evil).

Oops,

not a good plan, but remember—as agents of free will, we consciously or unconsciously are permitted to make good or bad choices.

We are vessels or channels either permitting good or evil—one or the other—so as agents of free choice, choose wisely.

Always remember, "We're a vessel to whomever we yield."

Just a note: Recalling when the two ladies and I went fishing, don't wait for the most challenging times as happened there—instead, you should practice binding and loosing in the right way every day, all the time.

CUTTING OFF THE ENEMY

Along with binding and loosing, we've been given the Power to cut off ALL the enemy and ALL the works of evil.

God said to David,

"I was with you wherever you went, and have CUT OFF ALL your ENEMIES from before you;" (2 Samuel 7:9)

"Draw up your battle lines against Babylon on every side, all you who bend the bow;

Shoot at her, do not be sparing with your arrows, for she has sinned against the Lord.

Raise your battle cry against her on every side!

For this is the vengeance of the Lord: Take vengeance on her; As she has done to others, so do to her.

CUT OFF the SOWERS FROM BABYLON and the ONE WHO WIELDS the SICKLE at the time of harvest." (Jeremiah 50:9–16)

Who is Babylon?

"She has become a resort and dwelling place for demons, a dungeon haunted by every loathsome spirit, an abode for every filthy and detestable thing.

I then heard another voice from Heaven saying, 'Come out from her, My people, so that you may not share in her sins, neither participate in her plagues.

For her iniquities (her crimes and transgressions) are piled up as high as Heaven, and God has remembered her wickedness and [her] crimes [and calls them up for settlement].'" (Revelation 18:2–5)

Babylon is a picture, an analogy of evil, representing what we're to cut off.

Henceforth, cut off ALL the enemy and ALL the works of evil.

The same goes for cutting off "the work of the soul", "curses", "curse-links", and "soul-ties."

THE WORK OF THE SOUL

Remember the discussion about "blessing and cursing?" When we agree with evil, we become a vessel, a channel for evil to spew through us, directed at whomever we are (knowingly or unknowingly) cursing.

As stated previously, maybe you never thought of it this way before, but it can be someone purposefully or ignorantly channeling curses and evil via the work (use) of their soul toward you and others.

How about giving the (hate-filled) finger or the 'ol "evil eye", "stink eye" or any other dirty and judgmental looks or actions? Have you ever gotten angry at anyone and said or thought some "not so nice" things about them? How about some people like politicians on TV? How about people at stores that annoy you? How about at church? How about anywhere?

How about when we judge or curse drivers, not just their driving abilities? There's a reason I mention them a lot.

How about when we judge, speak, or even think evil on someone or something for whatever reason—no matter if it's something they said—or actions done or not done—or the way they looked at us—or what we're convinced they are thinking?

These are just a few examples of the many, many, many works of the soul.

CURSE-LINKS

"Curse-links" can be "links" to people, objects, or things, that we allowed ourselves to become entangled with or people use to entangle us.

Unfortunately, while we have the ability to become entangled all on our own, others can evoke them via "praying" and/or putting curses over us by any means—until whatever time they deem fit—which might be "forever."

There are the obvious things: Like voodoo dolls, a lock of hair, a piece of clothing, something owned, taken, sent, or given to us are tangible objects that can used for such. They might not "pray" or send curses immediately—they might just wait until they get mad or judge that "we deserve it"—then release or invoke them at that time.

Recently I had a "run in" with a manager at a local grocery store—actually we were both at fault and very rude to each other. I know, hard for you to believe that I could be a "hot head." I won't go into the details, but words were said on both sides. I went home justifying myself, my words, and my actions.

Of course the Lord had another opinion. He told me to go apologize to the man for my part—but the manager had told me not to come back to his store—ever again—so I wrote an apology letter to him in case he threw me out upon return. When I came back another manager said he was at the store, but wasn't available at that moment, so I left the letter with her to give to him—which I'm sure she did.

The letter stated while we were both equally at fault for our own rudeness, words, and actions—I took 100 percent ownership of my faults and apologized for them. I left my name and phone number at the bottom in case he would ever want to make amends—not worrying if he would or not. It never happened.

Moving on, attempting to get to the point, you need to know another thing about me—I'm cheap. Yeah, so what—add that to my list. Therefore, I don't throw out much of anything and reuse everything I can—yes, even cheap plastic grocery sacks—which I have a MILLION, plus or minus, saved up by now—so I didn't need his bags—but as I said I'm cheap—so I kept them.

The interesting thing was that each time—after delivering the letter—as soon as I picked up one of that store's grocery sacks to use for whatever purpose—I'd feel the "curse-link" he'd (knowingly or unknowingly) put on it. It was his way of cursing me through his anger that anything that had to do with his store or that day would reign evil on me.

I could be wrong—it won't be the first time or the last—I'd never met nor seen this man before, but I sense that he's a Christian and even a leader, maybe even an elder, in his local church somewhere nearby—who has been thinking, speaking, and "praying" evil upon me (knowingly or unknowingly). Which the *god* of this world is *just loving the irony* of getting a Christian leader to be such a vessel for him.

Of course being the cheapskate I am, I didn't simply throw out those plastic bags. That's something that many might choose to do—hoping, assuming that would alleviate the curse—but when someone is channeling evil on you, most likely it won't.

A little tangent: For those who think that they can bury their head in the sand, like an ostrich, to AVOID GETTING ATTACKED by the devil—think again—when you're bent over with your head in the sand, you will be in the perfect position to get your ass kicked.

Okay, now I'm back.

So I'd forget between each use—and again, each time I touched one of those bags I'd immediately sense the curse—knowing the curse-link was there. At which time I'd just cut off the curse-link sending the "arrows" back to the archer (with no judgement or ill will towards him—not our job, remember?)—and go ahead and use them anyway. By the way, in case you're wondering, the curse would dissipate instantly. This happened repeatedly until they were all used and gone.

Cheap, stubborn, and maybe a little dumb—yup, that's me—just keep adding them to my list. Maybe you don't think this is funny, but I actually enjoy making fun of myself, as long as the Power of God is there and keeps the trouble far away.

Another example: Remember the old chain letters or derivations sent by mail or email? Nowadays potentially promoted in various ways via social media. All are curse-links. Why do you think people would get the "evil bad results" if they didn't pass them along in time as directed? Do you really believe that the chain letters or their derivations have power? They did not—and they do not—but the sadistic ruler of this world *does* and *he loves* to back this type of play.

Now let's take a look at less obvious examples.

One example is money.

While money is not evil in itself, but,

"The LOVE of money is A ROOT OF ALL KINDS OF EVIL."

And,

"It's through this CRAVING that some have been LED ASTRAY and have WANDERED from the FAITH and PIERCED THEMSELVES THROUGH with many acute [mental] pangs [pains, griefs]." (1 Timothy 6:10)

So, LOVING money allows a curse (empowered by the ruler of this earth) to attach itself to us and continuously bring evil on our lives—even if that only means keeping us from the Lord.

How about any of the other, "things that will take us down?" Unholy desires and other distractions such as pride, power, the misuse of sex, falling for religion and religiosity, or falling for anything that will take our eyes off the Lord.

When we fall for any of these pitfalls, it again allows a curse to attach itself to us and continuously bring evil on our lives.

Another large area of "curse-links" will be noted and explained in *The Atmosphere Around Us* section a couple chapters ahead.

SOUL-TIES

What are "soul-ties?"

Consider "the work of the soul" as "one offs"—one-time curses sent our way—which may or may not be repeated, depending upon the perpetrator.

"Soul-ties" are different. They're attachments ("soul links") that someone has cursed or tied to us indefinitely. These will remain in perpetuity unless and until the perpetrator decides to end it, which is unlikely, or we learn to cut them off.

Consider them the "many."

Typically, these types of attachments are based on someone wanting to curse someone else "forever" or at least a long, long time.

They expend a tremendous amount of energy yielding to evil.

They may or may not realize what they're doing.

The most obvious examples would be (white or black) witches casting incantations or spells on people or things. It also might be setting up "voodoo" type or (weird) "spiritual" type shrines purposed to "get," "effect," "change," or "hurt" someone—for the initiator's benefit—or out of anger wanting to invoke punishment.

Other obvious examples would be people consistently projecting hate, curses, unforgiveness, or judgements on others—but it could be many things.

Sometimes it could be as simple as someone praying evil upon you.

Oops.

Did I mean what I just said?

That even (good) Christians could be guilty of doing this? Praying evil?

Oh, absolutely; and far too often, Christians are the worst—because we're told to pray but haven't been taught the correct boundaries or how to pray correctly.

It's one of the "best" (great) deceptions the enemy plays on Christians.

Conscious of what they're doing or not, many good-meaning Christians fall into the "one offs" or "many" categories.

ATTACKS

Expanding from earlier, their "prayers" may be asking God to "deal with," "teach lessons to," or "get" another person—especially other believers—people that they're "judging," "unhappy with," or actually just "pissed off at."

In these cases, it many times will be portrayed to be under (the pretense of) spirituality. They'll use the guise of regular praying and/or gossip praying to invoke these things. (Remember, we can always pray against evil but not against people.)

While God the Father won't answer those prayers, there is the *god* of this world, the one with the little "g," that, when channeled, will.

Remember: "Christians are the only army that shoots its wounded."

It's sad to say, but (white or black) witches are actually more honest about who they are and what they do than Christians concerning these areas. The witches openly tell you they're going to curse you—whereas Christians cloak their misguided curses in false "spirituality" and "prayers."

As mentioned previously, we can "all of a sudden" feel attacked, fear, depression, oppression, anger and wrath, mentally sick, physically sick, or other ill feelings—all seemingly coming "out of nowhere."

In this light, it may very well be a spiritual issue, not a physical or psychological one.

It may be the "one offs" or the "many" works of the soul and/or soul-ties.

Over the years, I have many times felt these things coming against me and/or my family. Sometimes it may disorient me for a period of time—until the light bulb turns on.

When I realize what's happening—then cut it off—it dissipates almost immediately.

Why almost immediately?

Sometimes it is immediate.

Sometimes it takes a bit longer.

Sometimes it requires some prayer to realize where it's coming from and how the Father wants to end it. No matter what, it ends pretty quickly.

Anything that dissipates that rapidly confirms it was a spiritual condition, not a physical or psychological one.

ADDENDUM - JUST IN CASE YOU'RE WONDERING - NUMBER ONE

Numerous times through the years I've heard people praying, "Lord, I *ask* You to bind the (enemy/devil/spirit(s))" or repeating what the Old Testament angels would say, "The Lord rebukes you", thinking that's what we as believers should do—sorry—that's BS. Unfortunately spoken by folks who do not yet understand the New Testament Authority given by the blood of Jesus and the Anointing.

The Lord CANNOT—or at least, WILL NOT do it.

You say WHAT! WHY?

Because He gave US ALL Authority over ALL the enemy—therefore it's NOW OUR job—not His.

ADDENDUM - JUST IN CASE YOU'RE WONDERING - NUMBER TWO

Some have asked what type words should you say or have said to bind, loose, or do any of the other things directed at the enemy.

The answer is I won't tell you.

It's not about exact wording—it's nothing that should be verbatim—definitely nothing that should become rote. The answer is to study ALL the information presented here in the manual—learning it in the Presence of the Lord—then respond as the Spirit of God (the Anointing) flows through you in the moment.

It's knowing WHO you are—WHO you serve—WHO you are with—and then speaking in His Authority.

REMEMBER: "WE'RE A VESSEL TO WHOMEVER WE YIELD."

CHAPTER TWENTY-ONE

NO FALSE CHRISTS, NO FALSE PROPHETS, ETC.

NO FALSE CHRISTS

NO FALSE PROPHETS

NO WOLVES IN SHEEP'S CLOTHING

NO CHARLATANS

"FOR FALSE CHRISTS [MESSIAHS] and false prophets will appear and show [perform] great signs and wonders to lead astray [deceive], if possible, even the elect." (Matthew 24:24; Mark 13:22)

LET'S TALK FALSE CHRISTS

What is a false Christ?

Is it someone who goes around and says, "I'm Jesus Christ"?

How many people, especially believers, would be lead astray or deceived by that?

Not many, I hope, especially the elect (yielded believers).

Oh, but you say he or she is preforming signs and wonders. Okay, that might deceive a few more, but don't magicians do the same? Who knows, maybe he or she could influence some more—but probably, still not many in total.

What would deceive the many?

Do you remember the Greek definition for *Christ* is "the Anointing?"

So a *false Christ* is a *false anointing*.

NOW THAT'S A DIFFERENT STORY!

That's a RECIPE for disaster.

False anointings could deceive believers and, possibly, even the elect.

How is a false anointing created in or around a person? Who would empower such an anointing?

The *god* of this world, the deceiver, the one who loves to lie, manipulate, and lead astray the people of this world.

Don't you understand by now, as the most powerful being God ever created, he can manipulate a hell of lot? And what he cannot manipulate directly, he can direct his minions to do for him including preforming signs and wonders.

Do you remember when Pharisees accused Jesus of being Beelzebub (one of the many names for the devil)?

"The Pharisees said, 'It's by Beelzebub, the prince of demons, that he drives out demons.'" (Matthew 9:34)

We know that Jesus really did cast out demons.

So why would they say that?

Because they understood that the devil can simply command his demon underlings to come out of someone anytime he wants—immediately—all for "show and tell"—thereby, performing fake exorcisms and fake healings.

Now those are signs and wonders that might even deceive the elect.

How do we test for false anointings versus the real?

Once again, ONLY by THE PEACE of God that passes understanding.

Satan can fake a lot, but he cannot fake "THE PEACE."

In First John 4:1, we're told,

"Beloved, DO NOT BELIEVE EVERY SPIRIT, but TEST [analyze, examine] the SPIRITS to see whether they are FROM GOD..."

Now we know.

Evaluate it by THE WORD of God and HIS PEACE together.

NO FALSE PROPHETS

What is a prophet?

The word *prophet* breaks down into two parts—"pro" which means "forth" and "phet" which means to "speak"—therefore, the word *prophet* means to "speak forth."

The part of First John 4:1 I left out from above to address now was "Because many false prophets have gone out into the world."

In whole, it says,

"Beloved, DO NOT BELIEVE EVERY SPIRIT, but TEST [analyze, examine] the SPIRITS to see whether they are FROM GOD, because MANY FALSE PROPHETS have gone out into the world."

Ezekiel 13:3–6 says,

"This is what the Sovereign Lord says: WOE to the FOOLISH PROPHETS who follow their own spirit and have SEEN NOTHING!

Their VISIONS are FALSE and their DIVINATIONS a LIE.

Even though the LORD has NOT SENT THEM, They SAY, 'THE LORD DECLARES,' and expect Him to fulfill their words."

I was waiting to discuss false prophets here.

So, what is a false prophet?

He or she is someone under the influence of a false Christ (a false anointing).

Make sense?

FALSE ANOINTINGS CREATE FALSE PROPHETS.

A prophet of God, under God's Anointing, speaks forth the CURRENT WORD of the Living God.

Conversely, a false prophet speaks forth the deceptions of false Christs and false anointings.

"YOU WILL KNOW THEM BY THEIR FRUITS.

Every GOOD TREE bears GOOD FRUIT,

But the BAD TREE bears BAD FRUIT.

A GOOD TREE cannot produce BAD FRUIT,

Nor can a BAD TREE PRODUCE GOOD FRUIT...

Thus, by THEIR FRUIT, YOU WILL RECOGNIZE THEM." (Matthew 7:16–20)

Don't fall prey or believe everything you hear.

Once again, test it by THE WORD of God and HIS PEACE that passes understanding.

NO WOLVES IN SHEEP'S CLOTHING. NO CHARLATANS.

These two are pretty much the same as false prophets—just hiding under different pretexts—typically operating differently than a "prophet."

Therefore, they can be more deceptive and convincing to the masses simply by not declaring that they are "prophets."

Colossians 2:8 says,

"See to it that no one takes you captive

Through HOLLOW and DECEPTIVE PHILOSOPHY,

Which DEPENDS on HUMAN TRADITION

And the ELEMENTAL SPIRITUAL FORCES of this WORLD,

Rather than ON CHRIST [on the ANOINTING]."

Someone declaring themselves to be a "prophet" would and should receive more scrutiny.

Instead, these folks might portray themselves as "do-gooders," tugging at your heart strings, maybe wanting, begging for donations for some "worthy cause" that actually just lines their pockets.

Maybe a purveyor of missions—pushing some "spiritual-sounding" agenda.

Maybe a pastor, a teacher, a minister, or someone doing some "ministry from or for God." While sounding good on the surface it's built to lead you down the wrong path for any number of reasons.

While there are some good people doing some good things, there are evil-backed ones doing others.

Ephesians 4:14 tells us,

"We are NO LONGER to be CHILDREN, tossed here and there by waves,

And CARRIED ABOUT by every WIND of DOCTRINE,

By the TRICKERY of MEN,

By CRAFTINESS in DECEITFUL SCHEMING."

And in Matthew 7:15, we're told,

"BEWARE of the FALSE PROPHETS, who come to you in SHEEP'S CLOTHING,

But inwardly, are RAVENOUS WOLVES."

YOU WILL KNOW THEM BY THEIR FRUITS

"Not everyone who says to Me, 'Lord, Lord,' will enter the Kingdom of Heaven, but he who does the will of My Father who is in Heaven will enter.

Many will say to Me on that day, 'Lord, Lord,

Did we not PROPHESY, in YOUR NAME,

And, in YOUR NAME, CAST OUT DEMONS,

And, in YOUR NAME, PERFORM MANY MIRACLES?'

And then, I will declare to them, 'I never knew you;

Depart from me, you who practice lawlessness.'" (Matthew 7:21–23)

Don't mistake my concerns here.

There certainly are good people doing some of these functions or ministries for good, but here, we're differentiating the bad from the good in order to keep true believers from being deceived.

CHAPTER TWENTY-TWO

OPPRESSION VS. POSSESSION

FIRST, LET'S LOOK AT POSSESSION

D EMON POSSESSION OF MEN and women has been around since Satan and his demons fell from Heaven.

Let's look at several examples.

STARTING WITH A LEGION OF PIGS

In Luke 8:27–35,

"When Jesus stepped ashore, he was met by a demon-possessed man from the town. For a long time, this man had not worn clothes or lived in a house, but had lived in the tombs.

When he saw Jesus, he cried out, and fell at his feet, shouting at the top of his voice,

'What do you want with me, Jesus, Son of the Most High God? I beg you, don't torture (or destroy) me!'

For Jesus had commanded the impure spirit to come out of the man.

Many times, it had seized him, and though he was chained hand and foot and kept under guard, he had broken his chains and had been driven by the demons into solitary places.

Jesus asked him, 'What is your name?'

'Legion', he replied, 'because we are many', as many demons had gone into him.

And, they begged Jesus repeatedly not to order them to go into the Abyss (the waterless places).

A large herd of pigs was feeding there on the hillside.

The demons begged Jesus to let them go into the pigs,

And, He gave them permission.

When the demons came out of the man, they went into the pigs, and the herd rushed down the steep bank, into the lake, and all were drowned.

When those tending the pigs saw what had happened, they ran off and reported this in the town, and countryside,

And, the people went out to see what had happened.

When they came to Jesus, they found the man from whom the demons had gone out, sitting at Jesus's feet, dressed, and in his right mind."

In this case, this man was not being oppressed.

On the contrary, he was possessed internally by many demons all living on the inside as many as a Roman legion.

This man lived a tortured life from the inside out, and in one moment, Jesus set him free.

THE SEVEN SONS OF SCEVA

Then there were the Seven Sons of Sceva that we discussed in a previous chapter. In that chapter, our focus was on those who have Authority or not.

Here we'll focus on the demon possession. We saw,

"Some of the Jewish exorcists, who went from place to place, attempting to name over those who had EVIL SPIRITS [in them] (being DEMON-POSSESSED) the name of the Lord Jesus,

Saying, 'In the name of the Jesus whom Paul preaches, I command you to come out.'

Seven Sons of one Sceva, a Jewish chief priest, were doing this.

And, the EVIL SPIRIT [from the inside], answered and said to them,

'Jesus, I know, and I know about Paul, but who (in the hell) are you?'

And the man, in whom the EVIL SPIRIT RESIDED, leaped on them, subdued all of them, and overpowered them, so that they fled out of that house naked and wounded."

FORTUNE TELLING SLAVE

Another example is the,

"Fortune telling slave who had a SPIRIT by which SHE PREDICTED the FUTURE.

She followed Paul and the rest, shouting, 'These men are servants of the Most High God, who are telling you the way to be saved.'

She did this for many days.

Finally, Paul became so annoyed that he turned around and said to the SPIRIT, 'In the name of Jesus Christ I command you to COME OUT of HER!' At that moment the SPIRIT LEFT HER." (Acts 16:16–18)

There are many more. We won't take time to go into them all, but we will take the time to note here that all possessions are internal—demons, spirits residing on the inside, causing terrible anguish, pain, sickness, and damage in numerous areas or realms.

NEXT, LET'S LOOK AT OPPRESSION

Let's take a moment to differentiate oppression from possession.

Possession is from the inside out.

Oppression is from the outside in.

Psalm 89:22 says,

"The enemy will not deceive him, nor the son of wickedness [or the wicked] AFFLICT [or OPPRESS] him."

The word *afflict* in the Hebrew is 'anah' (aw-naw), which means "to be bowed (brought) down" or "afflicted," "afflict," "disturbed," "oppressed," "oppressors," "violate," "violated," "weakened," "ravished," "mistreated."

These words help enhance our understanding.

Oppression is not just,

The action of oppressing; arbitrary and cruel exercise of power.

The state of being oppressed.

A feeling of being weighed down in mind or body.

(*The American Heritage® Dictionary of the English Language*, fifth edition)

But it's also "being brought down," "afflicted," "disturbed," "violated," "weakened," "ravished," and "mistreated."

As true sadists and the author of sadism, these are just a part of the many things the enemy takes great pleasure in doing to us.

Luke 13:11–13 says,

"A woman was there who had been CRIPPLED by a SPIRIT for eighteen years.

She was bent over and could not straighten up at all.

When Jesus saw her, he called her forward and said to her, 'Woman, you are SET FREE from YOUR INFIRMITY.'

Then he put his hands on her, and immediately she straightened up and praised God."

Was that infirmity possession?

No.

Jesus did not tell the spirit to "leave" as he normally would when casting out demons—instead, He touched her, breaking the connection—disconnecting her from that external source of evil—which, in turn, immediately set her free from the imposed infirmity.

It was a spirit oppressing her, making her sick and crippled.

How about the time I listened to the tiny laughing voice? When I entertained (yielded to) it, giving permission, so it could oppress me—the resulting booming voice paralyzing me with fear.

Most of the time I believe that the Father wants to release His people from oppression, but does God ever allow it?

Yes.

God allowed Satan to oppress Paul with a "thorn in the flesh."

Was it physical? Mental? Spiritual? It really doesn't matter.

"To keep me from exalting myself, there was given me a thorn in the flesh, a MESSENGER of SATAN to TORMENT ME." (2 Corinthians 12:7)

Why?

So Paul wouldn't get a big head and think he had anything to do with the Power of God that flowed through him.

Now we can add "crippled," "paralyzed," "fear," "tormented," and "thorn in the flesh" to the words that describe oppression. All these can help us understand what spiritual satanic oppression can do to good people.

CAVEATS HANDLING POSSESSION AND OPPRESSION

So, what's our part, as believers, in handling possession and oppression?

FIRST, DEALING WITH POSSESSION

Remember the Seven Sons of Sceva playing exorcists?

Remember the movie, *The Exorcist?*

Both are excellent pictures of what NOT to do.

Instead, we saw how Jesus did it.

"'Be quiet!' Jesus said sternly. 'Come out of him!'

Then the demon(s) threw the man down before them all, and came out without injuring him."

NO entertaining them.

NO having big "discussions" with them.

NO antics.

NO show.

They have NO other option than to obey, INSTANTLY.

WHAT ARE SOME OF THE PITFALLS?

It's only recorded ONE time in the Bible, with "Legion," where Jesus asked demons their names.

And there, He did it to make a point about the vast number of spirits that were possessing the man (between five to six thousand—being the size of a Roman legion in that day)—before He allowed them to go into a herd of pigs and over the cliff.

In the early days, in our infancy, as we practiced "deliverance"—we did it because we could.

We'd ask them their names.

We'd have discussions with them.

We'd have arguments with them, telling them to leave—to hear them respond in GRUFF SATANIC VOICES echoing out of pretty young ladies (among others), "NO, you can't make me!" Watching them cause physical gyrations in and through the people—repeating over and over until they finally left.

From our ignorant perspective, it felt powerful to have that power over the enemy. It felt exhilarating, knowing we could talk to demons and, eventually, send them on their way.

But it was not right.

It gave the demons the attention they wanted.

It made them the "most important thing in the room." In that moment, it made them more important than the Lord.

Worse than that, it actually invoked fear into many believers standing around.

So even though the demons were eventually expelled, the enemy won MANY TIMES OVER.

HOW TO DO IT RIGHT

If the Lord wants us to do it, it's only because it's His will and the right time and the right place for that person.

Find out from the Lord if that's true before proceeding—or just don't do it.

Just because you can is NEVER enough.

Just because you can sense they're there is NEVER enough.

If it's God's will, then get clear discernment of what spirits are there and what's to be done—you don't need to ask them their names or what type they are—you'll know—or, most likely, you should've never been doing it anyway.

Again, you don't need to ask if you have Authority. Either you know you're under God's Authority and you have it—or not.

If they're talking, tell them to be quiet. Instruct them that they cannot talk or do anything at all, then simply tell them to leave.

No ifs, no ands, no buts.

No waiting.

No wailing.

No antics like The Exorcist.

No cross or holy water needed.

Just action, under Authority.

WHEN TO END POSSESSION

I'll repeat—if God isn't CLEARLY DIRECTING you to do it, then DON'T.

That's the clear definition of *the if and the when*.

Just because you're feeling your oats and now understand that "you've been given ALL Authority over ALL the enemy" is NEVER enough.

Maybe you want to prove how great you are (to yourself or others).

DON'T.

You will cause more harm than good.

NEXT, DEALING WITH OPPRESSION

That may be somewhat of a different story.

Yes, you've been given ALL Authority over ALL the enemy, but is that enough by itself?

Maybe not.

We still need to be listening to the Holy Spirit and operating under Authority.

So, when should we stop oppression?

Maybe often, maybe not.

We must be conscious of what God would have us do in each and every situation.

Never assume.

Never base it on past actions or experiences.

HERE'S THE RUB

When you finally grasp that you've been given ALL Authority over ALL the enemy, it's actually way too easy (in most cases) to end possession or oppression—minus exceptions. Remember Paul.

So, you ask, what's the problem with that?

Wouldn't it be doing everybody a BIG favor to get rid of and remove all the enemy from people or situations?

Maybe.

For about a HOT MINUTE!

Then HELL NO!

All removals must be backfilled with the Holy Spirit or, once again, just don't do it.

In Luke 11:24–26, we're told that,

"When an impure spirit comes out of a person, it goes through arid (waterless) places seeking rest, and does not find it.

Then it says, 'I will return to the house I left.'

When it arrives, it finds the house swept clean, and put in order.

Then it goes and takes seven other spirits, more wicked than itself, and they go in, and live there.

And, the FINAL CONDITION of that person is WORSE than the FIRST."

Not to be flippant, understanding Authority, kicking out (removing) a spirit from the inside or outside isn't the hard part.

That wasn't the issue Jesus was speaking about here.

The problem was when the spirit came back, it found "THE HOUSE SWEPT CLEAN," meaning nothing had replaced its previous occupation—it was empty. And according to God's Word, if empty, that spirit is (ABSOLUTELY) permitted to go round up seven other spirits, more wicked than itself, and they are all allowed to go in and live there.

There's only ONE singular solution—*IT MUST BE BACKFILLED*—and that backfill must be the Holy Spirit Himself.

The Holy Spirit is the ONLY thing that can fill the inside or around the outside to keep evil away.

That might not sound complicated or hard.

Remember binding and loosing?

Can't we just loose the Holy Spirit to fill in where the enemy was?

YES.

Then you ask, what's the big problem?

The problem is with the person receiving this newfound freedom—whether from possession or oppression—if they don't know, want, or receive the Holy Spirit to backfill these areas.

If they're not willing or ready for the backfill, then they won't choose nor give permission for Him to remain. The responsibility is on them to make that decision—they are the only ones who can do it—you cannot do it for them.

Therefore, the Holy Spirit will leave, and the multiplied spirits will return.

Thereby, the person's "FINAL CONDITION will be WORSE than the FIRST."

Hence, it becomes your responsibility to know the state of this person before you do anything.

If not, your "good works" weren't worth crap, and that person is screwed.

This is why we must know and operate within the will of God—no more, no less.

Don't ever get a big head like the disciples did, when they said,

"'Lord, even the demons are subject to us in Your name.'

And He said to them, 'Nevertheless, do not rejoice in this, that the spirits are subject to you, but rejoice that your names are written in Heaven.'" (Luke 10:17, 20)

Otherwise, once again, you might just be a child with a loaded gun, wondering why someone got hurt or killed.

THE ATMOSPHERE AROUND US

Another area of oppression or possession can be in the "atmosphere around us."

Have you ever felt an unexplainable "atmosphere," or "presence," around people, things, buildings, lands, or other?

Remember the ladies and I fishing? It can happen when someone walks up to you.

It also might happen when you walk up to them or when you just walk into a house, a building, a business, a room, a bathroom, or onto a property or piece of land. Then instantaneously feel an atmosphere of lust, fear, hate, anger, murder, confusion, sickness, or many other very negative or evil things in or around them—sometimes so thick you can "cut it with a knife."

These are a type of "curse-links" as we talked about previously. Where spirits can oppress or possess areas where they were allowed to gain entrance and control—and the more they were "given permission", the stronger the feelings will be.

All these things need to be cut off.

YIELDING TO THE ENEMY

Once again, "We're a vessel to whomever we yield."

Without question, as people of the earth, raised by the ruler of the earth, EVERYONE of US have AUTOMATICALLY, 100 PERCENT of the TIME, yielded ourselves to the enemy. From the time we were born, we were trained to do so—we knew no other way—there are NO exceptions—except one, JESUS.

Therefore from the beginning, we automatically opened doors for oppression or possession—so don't be surprised that you have or will need to deal with obtaining release from such in your life at some point in time.

After being born again, we mistakenly might think that problem ended "forever" simply by the Blood of Jesus and being SEALED by the Holy Spirit in that moment.

Unfortunately, NOT.

This will become clear in the future when we study the spirit, soul, and body.

The deep-rooted trainings in us are acutely engrained in our human nature and we will fall back and do those "yieldings" before doing anything else.

We have to learn new ways—a straight and narrow path as Jesus said.

Along that way we hopefully will learn to not yield to the enemy in new things, as well as, be retrained in the old—but remember those deep-rooted trainings in our "old man" will ALWAYS be our first and natural response. Thereby opening doors for oppression or possession again.

Therefore, if you haven't done this already,

Repent.

Ask for forgiveness.

Cut it off.

Close the doors, and choose to ask the Holy Spirit to come fill in.

CHAPTER TWENTY-THREE

ANGELS

TYPES OF ANGELS

I N THIS MANUAL, WE will discuss three types of angels: guardian, messenger, and warrior.

Each name defines their functions.

FIRST, GUARDIAN ANGELS

God puts His guardian angels around us to guard and protect His people.

As believers, we have them around us, protecting us, unaware.

"For He will command [give charge to] His angels concerning you to guard you in all your ways." (Psalm 91:11)

The word *guard* in the Hebrew is 'shamar' (shah-MAR), which means "to keep," "watch," "attend," "defend," "guard," "bodyguard," "observe," "preserve," and "protect."

WALKING TO WORK

There's a story I was told about a lady who lived in a very seedy and dangerous neighborhood. She had no car. Consequently, she had to walk from her home to work and back every day—afraid.

Walking to work in the mornings, she didn't feel as fearful because she was able to see up and down the alleyways; but each night, she lived in terror walking home at dark with dimly lit street lights.

She had no choice. She was forced to walk by many dangerous alleyways, many known as hides for the worst of the worst criminals in her city.

Every day as she traveled, fearing for her safety, she prayed for the Lord to protect her from these criminals.

For a long time, she taught herself to only look forward, trying to not glance into the alleyways on the way home. She knew if she did, she'd see the piercing eyes of many evildoers staring back at her. From time to time, even though she knew better, she still couldn't help herself and would glance that way.

After some time, she began to notice, passing by the alleyways, that the once piercing eyes of evildoers were now scared. She could see their eyes wincing with fear from the huddled corners.

This was strange.

This went on for months and months.

Unknowingly, her fear was subsiding.

Finally, her curiosity got the best of her.

One night, as she passed by, she gained the courage, walked up to the edge of one of the alleyways, and stopped. She called to one of the wincing set of eyes she'd seen many times before, huddled in the corner.

She asked him to come close.

Begrudging, slowly, he did.

When he finally came near, she asked, "Why do you and all the others who once seemed so frightening to me now seem scared and huddled in fear?"

The man exclaimed! "ARE YOU SERIOUS?"

"Anyone would be CRAZY to bother someone like you!"

"Walking up and down these streets, every day, with the two biggest bodyguards we've ever seen. Like the ones you've had on either side of you for months."

She prayed.

God answered.

And, put two BIG GUARDIAN ANGELS one on either side of her.

They walked alongside her every day.

Even though she couldn't see them, the enemy could.

THE VW VAN

Back in the day—yup, those same early Charismatic days—I was poorer than a church mouse. So was Bruce.

Someone had given Bruce an old worn-out, rickety 1960 VW van which he used for a while. Then he gave it to me. Neither of us had any money to fix it.

It wouldn't start without prayer first. It wouldn't run without prayer, nor would it stop without prayer.

You think I'm kidding? I'm not.

The engine was so bad that if you tried to start it, it would just turn over or click until the battery died, so instead, we knew that we had to pray for a good solid five to ten minutes before attempting to start it. Then when we had "The Peace", we turn it over, and instantly it started.

The brakes were so squishy that it never should have been driven on the road. If you (literally) stood on the brakes until they hit the floorboard, it might eventually stop.

But in faith, I drove it all the time.

You probably won't believe this, but numerous times when we didn't have gas, nor could afford to buy any, we'd sit there and pray. If it was the only transportation to get us somewhere we believed the Lord was sending us, He'd do miracles.

As we prayed, parked in the driveway, engine on or off, we'd watch the gas gauge rise from empty to a quarter tank or more until we had more than enough to get to our destination and back.

We used to have the *Christian Free Drive-In* in our city way across on the other side of town. Our city had over a million people, so not a small town by any means.

Every Saturday night, they'd play free Christian movies for Christians to enjoy and, hopefully, non-Christians to hear the gospel and be saved.

So, one Saturday night, we packed the van full of youth from the church and headed across town, taking the freeway. They all knew the drill:

Pray to start. Pray to stop.

When we got off that particular freeway, instead of it being a normal exit, it just turned into a regular city street. As we got off, I immediately realized the street was backed up with dead-stop traffic all the way to the traffic light.

Somewhat panicked, I quickly told them all to pray because I knew there was no way the van could stop in time.

I stood out of my seat, standing on the brake, which was fully depressed on the floorboard. The van was slowing a bit, but we were not going to be able to stop in time.

I watched in slow motion as we hit the station wagon in front of us.

I heard the loud crash.

I felt horrible.

Then some weird stuff happened.

First, the driver and the passengers in the station wagon very slowly turned around, like they'd heard an accident somewhere way off in the distance behind them. That was strange.

Second, instead of getting out of their car to see the damage and call the cops, per normal, when the light changed, they slowly drove off with everyone else ahead.

As I watched them drive off, I was in shock.

If you know anything about old VW vans, they have a flat nose. The engine is in the back, so the front of the van is a piece of sheet metal and a bumper away from the road or anyone else.

So, I had a perfect bird's eye view of the back of the station wagon in front of me when they drove off. I could see that there was *NONE—ZERO*—damage on it. Not the back of the wagon, not even a scratch on the bumper.

I pulled it over to the side of the road so other traffic could move on. Still in shock, we all got out of the van to find out what happened.

Even though there was no damage to the station wagon, the front of my van was totaled—totally crushed in—in the shape of a large body.

The only explanation, even though we could not see it, was that a large guardian angel stood in the gap between the station wagon and my van.

He (or she) left a big impression with all of us that night!

Once again, I humor myself.

SECOND, MESSENGER ANGELS

"Are not all angels MINISTERING SPIRITS sent to serve those who will inherit salvation?" (Hebrews 1:14)

God sent His angels to Daniel.

"A hand touched me and set me trembling on my hands and knees. He said to me, 'O Daniel, man of high esteem, understand the words that I am about to tell you, and Stand upright, for I have now been sent to you.'

'Do not be afraid, Daniel, for from the first day that you set your heart on understanding this and on humbling yourself before your God, your words were heard,

And, I have COME in RESPONSE to your words.'" (Daniel 10:10–12)

In addition to sending messengers to answered prayers, many times, we've entertained angels, unaware.

"Not neglecting to show hospitality to strangers, for by this some have entertained angels without knowing it." (Hebrews 13:2)

God sends these angels to us to deliver messages or help if and when and as He chooses.

Personally, I've met angels delivering messages from the Father three or four times, that I know of, over the years—mostly times when I needed to hear something from God, maybe because I wasn't listening too well otherwise, whether I knew it or not.

Every time, while in their presence, I felt something very supernatural and very stirring in my soul—all surrounded by His peace—times when as soon as they delivered their messages they disappeared, gone in an instant, something unmistakable, something beyond chance, something beyond the physical realm.

But it doesn't always need to be in bad times.

Just recently while in a good place I was at a Sam's gas station. After finalizing my gas, a feeble sweet little old lady (looked in her mid-eighties) on the other side of the pump asked me for help with her "Sam's gas transaction." As she stood there in front of her large SUV, she seemed befuddled on how to use her "new" Sam's card. The whole time I helped her, I noticed her amazingly sweet smile. As we locked eyes, I knew in that instant she was an angel. My smile back, said I knew; her return smile, said she was. Her sweet smile radiating The Presence of the Father was my word of encouragement that day.

Transaction completed, she started pumping her gas and thanked me. I got back in my car. I watched her as I drove off. I looked forward then back, and in a matter of three seconds, her large SUV remained, pump handle still inserted, but she was gone.

There was no one in the SUV.

So unless that feeble little old lady became a *Gold Medal Olympic sprinter* and cleared the half-empty large Sam's parking lot in a *matter of three seconds,*

then she was my messenger that day.

THIRD, WARRIOR ANGELS

"And, there was war in Heaven, MICHAEL and his ANGELS WAGING WAR with the dragon.

The dragon and his angels waged war, and they were not strong enough, and there was no longer a place found for them in Heaven.

And the great dragon was thrown down, the serpent of old who is called the devil and Satan, who deceives the whole world; he was thrown down to the earth, and his angels were thrown down with him." (Revelation 12:7–9)

Continuing with Daniel (from above), the messenger angel told him,

"The prince of the kingdom of Persia withstood me for twenty-one days;

Then behold, MICHAEL, one of the chief princes, came to help me." (Daniel 10:13)

Michael and his Warrior angels fought twenty-one days so that message could get to Daniel, afterward informing him of the ongoing fights.

"I shall now return to fight against the prince of Persia; and the prince of Greece." (Daniel 10:20)

GOD'S ANGELS ARE THERE FOR US, ALL THE TIME

Guarding us, as God's Messengers to us, as Warriors fighting for us.

GOD'S ANGELS ARE SPIRITS

As His creation, they have been given power beyond us, and they do a fantastic job, obeying the Father and protecting us, but is there any way that we can help under Authority?

Yes.

We'll address that more in the upcoming chapter, "THE STAND."

Remember, only God commands His angels. There we will see what we can do—of course, only within the four corners of God's will (His Word).

REAL FAITH, TRUE FAITH

R EPEATING WHAT I SAID earlier, when we're under God's Authority, the faith that He gives us is different—180 degrees different.

He doesn't want our faith. He doesn't want garbage faith. He doesn't want any kind of faith we can "muster up."

He doesn't want the "faithers" faith, who magically believe that if they try hard enough, they can proclaim "whatever" into being, who believe in rubbing the "genie in the bottle," and then get their "three wishes".

THIS IS THE WORK OF GOD

In John 6:28-29 it says,

"Therefore they said to Him, 'What shall we do, so that we may work the works of God?' Jesus answered and said to them, 'This is the work of God, that you **BELIEVE** in Him whom He has sent.'"

Have you ever noticed that this has an extremely significant double meaning?

DUAL MEANINGS ~ IT WORKS BOTH WAYS

First, it is *the Work of God* to reach us and it's *ONLY* by the Work of God that we **BELIEVE**.

Second, for us, *the ONLY Work of God that we can do* is to **BELIEVE**.

The first is more obvious, the second might not be.

SO WHAT DOES THAT MEAN?

If God didn't reach out to help us **BELIEVE** —we would NOT. We'd wander around this world doing our own thing—none the wiser. His Work of reaching out by Jesus coming and dying for us was going the ultimate distance. Then His continued Work by the Holy Spirit reaching out to us on a repeated basis is the utmost dedication and commitment for us to come to Him. This is the more obvious one.

The not so obvious one is that the *ONLY Work of God* we can do is to **BELIEVE**.

You say that doesn't make sense. We can do all kinds of things to Work the Works for God. We can study, pray, attend church, give tithes and offerings, preach the gospel, evangelize, teach, pastor, care for the flock, minister to one another, exercise all the gifts God gives us, disciple others, as well as, take care of our families, work our jobs as unto Him, etc., etc., etc.

Right?

Wrong!

The people did ask Jesus "What shall we do, so that we may work the works of God?" But Jesus did not answer that question. He did not tell them about all the "works" plural that they could or should do. Instead, His answer was "This is **THE WORK** of God." **THE WORK** is singular.

As Jesus said **THE WORK** is to **BELIEVE**. If we don't get this down then the rest of the "works" are just a total waste of time and energy. They won't impress the Father no matter what you do.

In John 9:4 it says,

"We must **WORK** the works of Him who sent Me as long as it is day; night is coming when no one can work.

I NEVER KNEW YOU

As stated previously from Matthew 7:21–23,

"Not everyone who says to Me, 'Lord, Lord,' will enter the Kingdom of Heaven, but he who does the will of My Father who is in Heaven will enter.

Many will say to Me on that day, 'Lord, Lord,

Did we not PROPHESY, in YOUR NAME,

And, in YOUR NAME, CAST OUT DEMONS,

And, in YOUR NAME, PERFORM MANY MIRACLES?'

And then, I will declare to them, 'I never **KNEW** you;

Depart from me, you who practice lawlessness.'"

And,

John 17:3 says,

"This is eternal life, that they may **KNOW** You, the only true God, and Jesus Christ whom You have sent.

The word **KNEW** and **KNOW** are the same word in the Greek 'ginōskō' (ghin-oce-ko), meaning "to come to know", "recognize", "perceive", "aware", "comprehend", "felt", "find", "found", "knew", "know", "knowing", "known", "knows", "learn", "learned", "perceived", "perceiving", "realize", "recognize", as well as meaning "virgin", "kept...a virgin".

In First Samuel 1:19 it says,

"Elkanah **KNEW** Hannah his wife, and the Lord remembered her."

Same goes for when "Cain **KNEW** his wife" in Genesis 4:17.

The word **KNEW** in the Hebrew is 'yada' (yah-DAH), meaning "to know", "becomes known", "knew", "known", "very well know", as well as, meaning to be "intimate", "cohabit", and "had relations".

Therefore, when Jesus said I never **KNEW** you, He meant in the deepest most intimate way.

We've been taught false religions and fake spirituality. We've been taught that if you try to be good and obey and do all these works for God, even with His gifts, that's like the "bees' knees", "the bomb", "the best" that anyone can be or do—EVER.

WRONG!

God does NOT care what great works you do for Him. He only cares if you **KNOW** Him in the deepest most intimate way—every moment of every day—and that begins with **BELIEVING** in Him.

SO HOW DO WE DO THAT?

BELIEVING in Him is an ACTIVE place of yielding to Him for CHRIST [the ANOINTING] to flow through us to bring us into the intimate Presence of God.

BELIEF IS FAITH IN ACTION

In Hebrews 11:1 it says,

"Now faith is the assurance (the confirmation, the title deed) of the things [we] hope for, being the proof of things [we] do not see and the conviction of their reality [faith perceiving as real fact what is not revealed to the senses]."

Faith in the Greek is from the root word 'peithō' (pay-tho), meaning "to have confidence", "assure or assurance", "convinced", "follow or followed", "persuade or persuaded", "put...trust", "put confidence", "relied", "seeking the favor", "trust", as well as, "listen", "obey", "obeying".

I love how faith is not only the assurance—but is also listening and obeying. Meaning we get the assurance after we listen and obey.

In Second Corinthians 5:7 it says,

"For we walk by faith [we regulate our lives and conduct ourselves by our conviction or **BELIEF** respecting man's relationship to God and divine things, with trust and holy fervor; thus we walk] not by sight or appearance."

And in Hebrews 11:3-13 it says,

"By faith we understand that the worlds were prepared by the Word of God, so that what is seen was not made out of things which are visible.

By faith Abel offered to God a better sacrifice than Cain...

By faith Enoch was taken up so that he would not see death...

And without faith it is impossible to please Him, for he who comes to God must **BELIEVE** that He is and that *He is a rewarder of **those who seek Him***.

By faith Noah...became an heir of the righteousness which is according to faith.

By faith Abraham, when he was called, obeyed...

By faith even Sarah herself received ability to conceive...

All these died in faith, without receiving the promises, but having seen them and having welcomed them from a distance..."

JESUS ONLY DID THE WILL OF THE FATHER

Again from Matthew 7:21 above,

"Not everyone who says to Me, 'Lord, Lord,' will enter the Kingdom of Heaven, but *he who does the will of My Father* who is in Heaven will enter.

In John 14:31 it says,

"But *I do as the Father has commanded Me*, so that the world may know (be convinced) that I love the Father and that *I do only what the Father has instructed Me to do*. [*I act in full agreement with His orders.*]"

In John 5:19 it says,

"Therefore Jesus answered and was saying to them, 'Truly, truly, I say to you, *the Son can do nothing of Himself, unless it is something He sees the Father doing*; for whatever the Father does, these things the Son also does in like manner.'"

In John 5:30 it says,

"*I can do nothing on My own initiative*. As I hear, I judge; and My judgment is just, because *I do not seek My own will, but the will of Him who sent Me*."

In John 7:38-39 it says,

"He who *BELIEVES* in Me, as the Scripture said, *'From his innermost being will flow rivers of living water.' But this He spoke of the Spirit*."

In John 8:29 it says,

*"And He who sent Me is with Me; He has not left Me alone, **for I always do the things that are pleasing to Him**."*

In John 8:55 it says,

"And you have not come to know Him**, but I KNOW Him and keep His word**."

This word *KNOW* in the Greek is 'oida' (oh-da), and is similar to 'ginōskō' (ghin-oce-ko) above, meaning "to have seen or perceived, hence to know", "become learned", "knew", "knowing", "understand".

Meaning it's out of this deep intimate relationship with the Father that Jesus **KNEW** Him and therefore ONLY functioned out of that **BELIEF**—that issues Real and True Faith—seeing and doing ONLY what the Father was doing.

WHAT IS THE WILL OF THE FATHER?

In John 6:38, 40 it says,

"For I have come down from heaven, **not to do My own will, but the will of Him who sent Me**.

For **this is the will of My Father**, that everyone who beholds the Son and **BELIEVES** in Him will have eternal life."

In John 14:11-14 it says,

"**BELIEVE** Me that I am in the Father and the Father is in Me; otherwise **BELIEVE** because of the works themselves.

Truly, truly, I say to you, he who **BELIEVES** in Me, *the works that I do, he will do also*; and greater works than these he will do; because I go to the Father.

Whatever you ask **IN My name**, that will I do, so that the Father may be glorified in the Son. If you ask Me anything **IN My name**, I will do it."

DOING THE WILL OF THE FATHER

I want you to catch something not commonly taught in the churches. When we hear that scripture, we unfortunately fall back to the "genie in the bottle" mentality again. We think there's some sort of magic to say *"In the Name of Jesus"* and whatever we say will be done—NOPE—SORRY—*not true at all*—NEVER EVER will be TRUE.

Do you remember what we previously learned about being *"In Christ"* about being *"In the Anointing"*? It's positioning ourselves inside of the Anointing and the Anointing in us. How does that happen? By 100 percent yielding to Him [which can ONLY be enabled by the Spirit of God in that moment—meaning we cannot even do that on our own] and then making the choice to get out of the way to allow the Spirit of God to flow through us.

Therefore, to be *"IN My name"* is to be *"IN Christ"*. From that position and that place ALONE will "whatever we ask" be done.

Oh, so as long as we get to that place we can ask for WHATEVER, right?

Oh, how COOL!

Unfortunately, NOT!

Are you going to blow my bubble again?

Yup!

Why?

Because when we get into that place *"IN Christ"*, we're no longer walking, doing, saying what we want—just like our older brother Jesus—we're walking, doing, and saying what we see the Father doing and saying.

Jesus ONLY did the will of the Father which was to **BELIEVE** in Him. By doing so He lived and operated out of the intimate Presence with the Father.

This is the definition of Real, True Faith.

It's not what you do. It's not how hard you try to believe (on your own). It's not anything you can EVER say. There's no rules or laws you can do. There's no magic formula anyone can give you.

Now can you begin to understand what is **THE WORK** of God? That we **BELIEVE.** And after we **BELIEVE**—then and only then—can we **BELIEVE** and operate out of the Real, True Faith that is issuing from God, in that moment alone, through the Holy Spirit from deep within.

100 PERCENT YIELDING TO HIM

As mentioned, above, that level can ONLY be enabled by the Spirit of God in each moment—[meaning we cannot even do that on our own]—and then making the choice to get out of the way to allow the Spirit of God to flow through us.

But I want to bring more clarity here. Each of us are at our own level with the Lord according to where we are in our journey with Him—*Everyone is different.* Therefore, my 100 percent might be a different requirement for me versus what 100 percent might look like and be the requirement for someone else. There are NO comparisons to be made between each other. The ONLY comparison is to Jesus—where we stand in Him—how much we are yielding to Him—and where we need to grow.

Again from Hebrews 11:6 it says,

"But **without faith [current living active belief]** *it is impossible to please Him.* For whoever would come near to God must *[necessarily]* **believe** that He is and that *He is the rewarder of those who earnestly and diligently seek Him [out]."*

And in Luke 12:48 it says,

"For everyone to who much is given, of him shall much be required; and of him to whom men entrust much, they will require and demand all the more."

Therefore, we must all stand and be accountable before God and to Him alone for what we've been given and where we are in this journey in this testing ground called earth. Not ourselves—Not others—Just Him.

BELIEVING IS "WHAT WE DO"

As taught earlier, YES, Choice and Yielding are the ONLY powers we have—but **BELIEVING** is the ONLY **Work** we can do to work the works of God.

Hopefully, now, you have a new understanding what **BELIEVING** means. In that light, does it put a new twist on when we call ourselves **"BELIEVERS"** who we're supposed to be? Not just *"believing in God"*. Not just *"Christians"*. But Real True **BELIEVERS** actively living a life of Real True Faith walking with our God.

BOTTOM LINE

If you do not approach your walk with the Lord in Real True Faith being an active living moment-by-moment **BELIEF**, then your walk will fail.

In the same way, if you do not approach your Standing in the Lord in Real True Faith being an active living moment-by-moment **BELIEF**, then your Stand will fail.

Please note: I'm once again NOT talking about creating perfection in ourselves EVER—it has nothing to do with us, our abilities, or how "religious" or "spiritual" we could EVER be. I'm talking about a life of **YIELDING, CHOICE**, and **BELIEVING**.

CHAPTER TWENTY-FIVE

THE STAND–PUTTING IT ALL TOGETHER

GOOD NEWS AND BAD NEWS

As the old saying goes, I've got some good news and some bad news. Which would you like to hear first?

THE GOOD NEWS

If you've taken the time to read and study everything up to this point, then you've given yourself a chance—an opportunity—to learn how to Stand.

Why do I say it that way?

Deuteronomy 29:29 says,

"The SECRET THINGS BELONG to the LORD our God,

But the things REVEALED to US, BELONG to US, and our children, forever."

If you live in my or others' revelation, you're doomed to fail.

You need to spend time with the Father, the Son, and the Holy Spirit to make ALL of this your own revelation.

Otherwise, you may be set up to get your ass kicked.

THE BAD NEWS

If you jumped ahead without reading and learning ALL up to this point, let alone making it your own revelation, then you're already set up for total absolute failure.

Remember the Seven Sons of Sceva.

So if you did jump here, go back and read the chapter on "THE FORMULA AND 'MAGIC' PRAYERS" before proceeding.

MOVING ON, PAST THE WARNINGS

THE DAILY STAND

Why daily?

Why not!

Aren't we told to pray unceasingly? Then why not Stand on a daily basis?

In Matthew 6:34 (AMP) we're told,

"So do not worry or be anxious about tomorrow, for tomorrow will have worries and anxieties of its own. Sufficient for each day is its own trouble.

Or, I do enjoy this one in the King James Version, where it says,

"Take therefore no thought for the morrow: for the morrow shall take thought for the things of itself. Sufficient unto the day is the evil thereof (or there in)."

I like to take this verse one step further.

"Sufficient unto the MOMENT is the evil thereof (or there in)."

It's time we understand that the enemy does NOT take a day off or a moment off—therefore, neither should we.

So since we're told to pray unceasingly, then why not Stand in every moment of every day?

If it was up to us by our capabilities we could never do it. But if we live in the Spirit and out of the Presence of God, we can.

Now let's learn how to Stand.

FIRST LESSON—YIELDING

Yield yourself to the Lord.

You have ZERO ability or power in yourself.

You can do NOTHING in the spiritual realm.

So yield yourself as a vessel, a channel for the Oil, the Anointing, to flow through you.

This will ALWAYS BE FIRST.

SECOND LESSON—GET YOUR INTERNAL HOUSE IN ORDER

Go back and study to do whatever it takes to get your FOUNDATIONS, KEYS, and other trainings in order—before you proceed to STAND. At least to whatever degree the Holy Spirit has revealed or will reveal to you at each point in your life.

THIRD LESSON—STANDING

In the scriptures, are we told to STAND?

Zechariah 4:14 says,

"These are the TWO (sources of) ANOINTINGS [again in the Hebrew, is 'yitshar' (yeets-hawr), meaning, 'fresh Oil', 'Oil', 'Anointed', 'Anointing'] who are STANDING by the Lord for the whole earth."

Standing in the Hebrew is 'amad' (aw-mad), meaning "to TAKE ONE'S STAND," "to STAND."

Second Corinthians 1:21 says,

"Now it is God who makes both us and you *STAND firm in CHRIST [the ANOINTING].*"

Exodus 14:13 says,

"Do not be afraid. *STAND firm and you will see the DELIVERANCE the LORD will bring you today.*"

Job 11:13–15 says,

"If you devote your heart to Him and stretch out your hands to Him, then you will lift up your face; *you will STAND firm and WITHOUT FEAR...*"

Psalm 20:6–8 says,

"Now this I know: *The Lord GIVES VICTORY to those with HIS ANOINTING ... WE RISE UP and STAND firm.*"

Proverbs 10:25 says,

"When the storm has swept by, the wicked are gone, *but the RIGHTEOUS STAND firm FOREVER.*"

Isaiah 7:9 says,

"*If you do NOT STAND firm in YOUR FAITH, you will NOT STAND at ALL.*" [This again from the NEGATIVE perspective.]

Luke 21:18–19 says,

"*STAND firm, and you will WIN LIFE.*"

Win in the Greek is 'ktaomai' (ktah-omh-a-hee), which means "acquire," "acquired," "gain," "get," "obtain," "possess."

First Corinthians 15:57–58 says,

"*He gives us the VICTORY through our LORD JESUS CHRIST [the ANOINTING].* Therefore, my dear brothers and sisters, *STAND firm.*"

First Corinthians 16:13 says,

"Be on your guard; *STAND firm in the FAITH;*"

Second Corinthians 1:24 says,

"Because it is *BY FAITH YOU STAND firm.*"

Galatians 5:1 says,

"It was for freedom that *CHRIST [the ANOINTING] set us free; therefore, KEEP STANDING firm.*"

Colossians 4:12 says,

"Wrestling in prayer for you, *that you may STAND firm in ALL the WILL of GOD, mature and fully assured.*"

Second Thessalonians 2:14–15 says,

"*He called you to this through our gospel,* so then, brothers and sisters, *STAND firm.*"

James 5:7 says,

"You too, *BE PATIENT and STAND firm.*"

Romans 5:2 says,

"Through whom we have *gained access BY FAITH into this GRACE in which WE NOW STAND.*"

Mark 11:25 says,

"And *when you STAND PRAYING, if you hold anything against anyone, forgive them.*"

AND FINALLY, DO ALL YOU CAN DO TO STAND, THEN STAND

"Therefore, *put on the full armor of God, so that when the day of evil comes, you may be able to STAND your ground,*

"And *AFTER you have done EVERYTHING to STAND firm, STAND firm.*" (Ephesians 6:13–14)

Is this enough?

We could go on.

Are you convinced yet that God wants us to Stand? That Standing is an important function, and that action is to be a dynamic part of our lives?

HOW TO STAND

So, building on all we've reviewed to this point, let's discuss how to Stand.

FIRST, YIELD YOURSELF TO THE LORD

Enough has been said to this point—over and over.

NEXT, RESIST THE ENEMY

Remember, resisting then fleeing only happens when done in order.

"*HUMBLE* yourselves. *SUBMIT* yourselves to God. *RESIST* the devil, and *he WILL FLEE* from you." (James 4:6–7)

And,

"*Resist him, STANDING firm in the faith.*" (1 Peter 5:8)

NEXT, NO ROTE

Anything we do can easily turn to rote—"a memorizing process using routine or repetition, often without full attention or comprehension" (quoted from *The American Heritage Dictionary of the English Language*, fifth edition).

Repeating actions or words, may be fine in our daily responsibilities. *In PRAYER, in STANDING, it's NOT.*

It's way too easy for our prayers and Stand to turn to rote—just repeating some words that no longer have a true or current meaning, *becoming something of ZERO value, no longer coming from your heart, and the Presence of God.*

If they're not current and not from the Presence of God, *then they will be empty, having NO Power or Authority behind them.*

So be mindful.

Continuously watch out for this problem.

NEXT, JUST DO IT!

AREAS TO COVER IN YOUR STAND

RAISE UP MORE THAN ENOUGH PEOPLE

Asking the Father that He *raise up more than enough people* (believers) that will *Stand*—more than enough *Standing together in every moment of every day.*

Joshua 23:10 says,

"One of your men puts to flight a thousand, for the Lord your God is He who fights for you, just as He promised you."

And Deuteronomy 32:30 says,

"One man [can] chase a thousand, or two [can] put ten thousand to flight."

WHAT IF WE HAD EVEN MORE BELIEVERS STANDING?

If two can put ten thousand to flight, then what could three believers do?

How about five?

How about ten?

How about one hundred?

How about one thousand?

How about one million?

How about more?

Pray it be so!

AND, IN THIS, WE AGREE

Speaking into the universe, *stating before the heavens and the earth* that *the BEST of all Stands is duplicated* from day to day, moment by moment, *whether said correctly or not.*

This means God knows our hearts. He knows what should be said and when and how to say it correctly in that moment and, fortunately, not depending on us or our "perfection."

Providing coverage in each and every moment of every day by *speaking forth* in the Name of Jesus—*the Light, the Truth, and the Blood.*

Agreeing that we all agree in this, speaking into the universe, *stating before the heavens and the earth* that there is constant coverage for:

ALL of us that are Standing together.

For our families, homes, jobs, businesses, finances, etc.

For ALL we have stewardship over.

For ALL the people and things we pray for.

For ALL the people and things God would have us *Stand* for.

For EVERY ripple effect that affects our lives.

Binding up ALL the enemy and ALL evil, *loosing* the Holy Spirit and ALL good.

Speaking into the universe, *stating before the heavens and the earth* that there's NO coverage (ever) for:

False Christs.

False prophets.

Wolves in sheep's clothing.

Charlatans.

Or anyone or anything allowing evil to rule over and/or flow through them in any way.

Speaking into the universe, *stating before the heavens and the earth* that this *Stand* covers the past, the present, and the future—meaning it's not up to us to figure out any timing issues—or if we said it in the correct manner or the exact right time or not, that's God's job, not ours. Remember He's not limited by time.

ALL POWER OVER ALL THE ENEMY

Recognizing and receiving that we were given ALL Power over ALL the enemy, therefore *binding up* ALL the enemy in every way in the heavens and the earth for ALL time—anything trying to come against us, directly or indirectly, through any people or things.

Not allowing evil to be released through any curses, incantations, spells, or any other channels that might come against any of us or the people and things we *Stand* for—that the oppressive enemy around us or would come around us—*that the Lord would have sent away—is to go to the waterless places* and *stay there* (and are *not allowed* to come back)—and *asking, loosing, and receiving* the Holy Spirit to *come and backfill* ALL these areas.

ANGELS

Standing, loosing His angels ALL around us—guardian angels, messenger angels, and warrior angels. And because the enemy is bound and will remain that way, *releasing* His angels to do ALL the Father wants them to do *to protect us—deliver the Word of the Lord to us—including releasing* His warrior angels to be able to take out and destroy the enemy from the heavens and the earth.

Father, we appreciate that You place Your angels round about us, and we appreciate the angels, Your servants, are protecting, speaking, and fighting for us.

THE BLOOD

Placing the Blood of Jesus over us, as a spiritual mirror, as a dome of protection that *stops* ALL ARROWS and ALL WEAPONS (of any type) sent against us and (*reflecting*) *sending* ALL such things back to those who sent them against us to take out ALL evil.

Cutting off the work of the soul, curses, curse-links, and soul-ties, and once again, *sending* those things back to those who sent them against us to take out ALL evil.

In sending these things back, *we are not to pray evil upon them.* Instead, *we are cutting off the evil behind them so we are protected.*

We are to *come from an attitude of blessing* and that the "blessings" are to be given by the Lord with their own ARROWS and WEAPONS returning on them so that it might help them to repent and be saved.

Please remember, this is a very delicate, thin line to walk, *so keep your heart supple before the Lord.* If His Peace seems to "flutter" in you at times—especially as if something "does not seem right" in the middle of any of these prayers—*that's a signal.*

It should be a clear sign to you to STOP then ASK how you should be praying and WAIT until His Peace returns.

Then when you understand what to do, repent, apologize, correct, and redirect.

REPENTING OF OUR SINS

Always repent of your sins including any cursing, (wrong) judgments, or unforgiveness—*then ask* for His Forgiveness, Mercy, and Grace.

BLESSINGS, WITHOUT CURSING

Continually praying blessings without cursing in ALL things including *removing* (wrong) judgements and unforgiveness from our midst.

This is a hard one, as we discussed earlier, but it must be repeated.

Remember how God blesses. We're to *pray against evil, not people.* Therefore, in our *Stand*, we are to *cut off evil and then pray blessings* ['barak'], understanding and leaving it up to God to do WHATEVER it takes. Also understanding and *praying those who bless us will be blessed* ['barak'], and *those who curse us will be cursed*—meaning we're *speaking* into the universe, *stating before the heavens and the earth* that it's God's job to resolve those things, not ours.

We need to continuously pray that God teaches us how to pray here.

RELEASE AND RECEIVE FOR EVERY REALM

For every realm about us—whether it's the spiritual, physical, mental, emotional, financial, and/or any other realm—we *continually ask for, release, and receive* His blessings, healings, miracles, provisions, and protection in every area of our lives, in every moment of every day—everything that Jesus completed at the cross.

For every realm about us and every realm within us, we *cut off* every negative affect, every negative growth, every negative attack, every tumor, cancer, sickness, and disease that can happen in any of these realms.

And *pulling down* ALL vain imaginations and high and lofty thoughts from us, everyone we *Stand* for, and every ripple effect that can ever affect our lives in any way for ALL time and taking all these things captive into the obedience of CHRIST.

BINDING UP AND CUTTING OFF

We *bind up and cut off* ALL evil and evil ones in the heavens and the earth. We *Stand*, taking out ALL evil, *by the Blood of Jesus* in ALL ways and at ALL times.

We *Stand, loosing* the Holy Spirit in every area and in every way.

IN THE NAME OF JESUS

Speaking forth, in the Name of Jesus,

the Light, the Truth, and the Blood.

Speaking Light into darkness, causing it to go into confusion, disruption, and destruction.

Causing darkness to flee, at the speed of light.

Causing evil to turn on one another and destroy one another like in the days of Jehoshaphat.

Causing them to circle on one another and fire on each other until destroyed—knocking down their house of cards—and like rats fleeing from a sinking ship, they will turn on one another and destroy one another, thinking they will save themselves in the end, but they will not.

FALSE CHRISTS, FALSE PROPHETS

Expose and remove ALL false Christs, false prophets, wolves in sheep's clothing, charlatans, and ALL other people yielded to evil from every position of government, authority, leadership, and power in the Church and the earth.

Taking ALL their power, control, and money (which is also influence and power) from those yielded to evil in the Church and the earth.

Let everyone see the evil,

hate it, and turn from it.

Removing ALL those who are yielded to evil from every position of leadership, power, and influence in the Church and the earth.

Putting true, good, yielded, conservative believers in charge of every level of government, *raising up* true conservative believers as our leaders in every level of every government everywhere—those that will *undergird the people and raise them up* in the Church and the earth.

Blessing those true, good, yielded, conservative believers to obey the Lord and do right.

Removing evil ones, and putting all such good leaders to remain in place until Your next coming.

Turn the world around. *Turn* our lives around. *Turn* the economy around. *Turn* everything around—for Your people.

PRAYING BLESSINGS ON OUR FAMILIES

Praying the Father would bless us as individuals, families, groups, homes, jobs, businesses, finances.

Stopping ALL attacks coming against us at ALL times and in ALL ways.

Blessing us in ALL ways.

Healing us in ALL ways.

Keeping us safe in ALL things.

Keeping His angels round about us at ALL times.

Blessing our families, our homes, our jobs, our businesses, and ALL that we have stewardship over. *Turning ALL things around*, and making them wonderful as we see them on top of how He sees them—and the *same for ALL those who Stand with us.*

Then taking the time to specifically *pray and Stand* for ALL our individual family members—their needs (in all realms), their jobs, their businesses, etc.—also doing the same for ALL the prayer needs of ALL the saints that would be *Standing* together now or in the future.

ONCE AGAIN, NOT BASED ON US

Based on, the Name of Jesus and His Authority ALONE.

Never based on anything in us, recognizing that there is NO power in us.

Instead, that ALL the POWER of the universe resides in Christ, who is in us as the Anointing, the Fullness of the Godhead, now seated at the Right Hand of the Father.

THIS IS A TEMPLATE, ONLY

What you've just been given here is a template and summation of the things outlined in this manual for you to be able to Stand.

THIS IS NOT TO BE DONE VERBATIM.

IT IS NOT TO BE DONE IN ROTE.

THIS IS NOT TO BE DONE WITHOUT HIS REVELATION.

IT IS NOT TO BE DONE WITHOUT HIS AUTHORITY.

You *MUST* slow down and take the time to study and learn ALL these things before the Lord—to get them into your heart as His REVELATION to you and the release of His AUTHORITY—then you will see and know how to use it.

Or you will be defeated and get the $hit kicked out of you like the Seven Sons.

REMEMBERING THE SECRETS

WE NEED HUMILITY

Not pride as we talked about earlier.

Never forget the Seven Sons of Sceva.

Do not forget that even true yielded believers, who should know better, can get their asses kicked—such as Dick did "feeling his oats" and taking on the "Blue Devils." We need to learn and remember so we don't make the same mistakes.

WE'RE ALL PART OF THE ARMY OF GOD

Therefore, *STAND TOGETHER*.

We must yield to the Lord and work together with ALL the believers that will fight with us, alongside us.

DO NOT LOOK for divisions.

DO NOT LOOK where we might disagree.

DO NOT LOOK to "shoot the wounded."

Instead, *pray to agree, WHEREVER we can agree, in the Spirit.*

Ecclesiastes 4:12 says,

"And though a MAN might prevail against him who is alone, TWO will withstand him, and a THREEFOLD CORD is NOT quickly broken."

Matthew 18:19 says,

"Again I say to you, that if TWO of you AGREE on EARTH about ANYTHING that they may ask, IT SHALL BE DONE for them by My FATHER who is in Heaven."

Typically, we think of that verse when we're physically together, praying in a group or at a church.

Nowadays, we probably imagine that to also be true in a virtual world of phones or internet.

IN THE LIGHT OF PRAYER

PRAYER HAS *ALWAYS* BEEN VIRTUAL.

Two or more can pray, whether together or not.

Whether knowing they're praying together or not.

Believers, knowingly or unknowingly, can pray in *UNISON* with each other *simply by YIELDING to the Holy Spirit and following His direction.*

Ephesians 6:18 says,

"And *pray in the Spirit on all occasions* with all kinds of prayers and requests. With this in mind, be alert and always keep on praying for all the Lord's people."

Romans 8:26–27 says,

"In the same way the Spirit also helps our weakness; for we do not know how to pray as we should, but *the Spirit Himself intercedes for us with groanings too deep for words*; and He who searches the hearts knows what the mind of the Spirit is, *because He intercedes for the saints according to the Will of God.*"

PUTTING THE ENEMY TO FLIGHT

One can put a thousand to flight, and two can put ten thousand to flight.

So, what could be done if we had three, five, ten, one hundred, one thousand, one million, or even more believers Standing together?

WITH THAT THOUGHT IN MIND

Can you begin to comprehend why the devil wants infighting among us?

Why he wants an army that shoots its wounded?

Why he wants us to gossip or pray evil on others?

Why he wants divisions and denominations separating us?

Why he wants us f—ed up by judgement, unforgiveness, and cursing?

Why he wants to get us off course by a few degrees? In any which way?

Why he wants distractions?

Why he wants us living in sin, without repentance?

And why he wants any other thing that would keep us from the Lord?

Let alone learning how to Stand.

Then doing it properly and together in UNISON?

ADDENDUM ~ MY TWO CENTS WORTH

Along with being a believer, husband, father, and businessman, I'm politically active.

I want to take a moment to state I believe that ALL Christians should be involved in the things of Heaven and of earth. Not only STANDING and praying but in working, taking care of our families, handling our responsibilities, and voting—yes, voting.

We all need to find the balance.

Part of what we should be doing, is STANDING and PRAYING, for OUR LEADERS in the EARTH, as well as, the CHURCH.

I'm not going to tell you how you should believe or vote.

I will say we should be STANDING and PRAYING for True Conservative Christian leaders to be raised up in every level of government in the Church and the earth.

There are well-meaning Christians who give "spiritual," "religious," or even secular reasons why not to vote; and while they have free choice, I believe they're wrong—very wrong.

We should be doing our due diligence and vote. It is part of our earthly responsibilities.

Then some will say, "Why waste my time and vote? You know it's all rigged. You know elections have been stolen. So, why waste anyone's time?"

They are correct.

It has been rigged many times. Yes, elections have been stolen.

Now you say, "He's part of the conspiracy theorists."

Nope. I'm a realist.

Also, I've been a programmer for over forty years, and I know how "dirt easy" it is to cheat with computers. Voting machines, tallying machines, central "data collection" machines, at any level, are all computers. Most, if not all, running hidden and encrypted software.

I also know that I, along with many thousands of other decent programmers here in the USA or from around the world, can easily write algorithms—algorithms that can "hide themselves" inside any of those systems and "cheat all day long" with or without internet connections.

So, back to the cynics' points of view. Why vote?

Because we have a Secret!

What's this manual about?

STANDING.

So, wake up and do your job for yourself, your family, your friends, other believers, the Church, and the world.

Stand every day "In the Name of Jesus," *speaking forth and releasing*, "the Light," "the Truth," and "the Blood."

Speaking forth the Light to reveal, expose, and destroy ALL evil and darkness working in or behind people, systems (things), groups, the Church, and the world.

Speaking forth the Truth to reveal, expose, and destroy ALL the lies working in or behind people, systems (things), groups, the Church, and the world.

And *speaking forth the Blood* to cover and protect us, ALL we have stewardship over, and ALL the good people and things God would protect in the Church and the world.

So, do your JOBS!

ALL of them.

Do NOT be a "spiritual ostrich" burying your head in "spiritual sounding" sand with your ass in the air ready to be kicked.

If we do Stand, then cheating, lying, deceptions, rigging or stealing elections, government corruption, hidden world agendas to subvert nations, etc., etc., etc. can be exposed and, hopefully, prayerfully, be intervened on the spiritual as well as the physical level to be stopped, reversed, and corrected for ALL the days before His Second Coming.

ADDITIONAL SIDENOTE

In case you haven't figured it out by now, we do not battle against flesh and blood, as stated in the "FOREWORD."

"For though we walk (live) in the flesh, we are not carrying on our warfare according to the flesh and using mere human weapons."

Remembering,

229

"For the weapons of our warfare are not physical [weapons of flesh and blood], but they are mighty before God for the overthrow and destruction of strongholds (or fortresses)."

For those of us who care what's happening to our country and around the world, the open infiltration of Marxism, Socialism, Communism, and the ilk into our countries, governments, societies, education of our children, daily lives, and yes, even our churches, perpetrated by the Liberals, Progressives (sorry if that offends some), Marxists, Socialists, Communists, Globalists, Satanists, and all the "axis of evils" in the world—*who do you think is behind ALL of them?*

As stated previously from Ephesians 6,

"For our struggle is not against flesh and blood, but against the rulers, against the authorities, against the powers of this dark world and against the spiritual forces of evil in the heavenly realms."

By now you should know, it's the ruler of this world. He's the evil influencing, backing, and empowering such, so when we think we're battling against these earthly entities—*we're not—we're battling against the PURE EVIL behind them.*

While we are to do all we can do to help end such, in every realm and in every way, how do we actually stop these entities' reign of terror?

First, before doing anything else—*by STANDING*—STANDING will cut the legs off from underneath them.

By binding up and cutting off all the evil behind ALL these entities and the people promoting such, *SPEAKING FORTH and RELEASING,* "In the Name of Jesus," "the Light," "the Truth," and "the Blood." *Then SPEAKING CONFUSION, DISRUPTION, and DESTRUCTION into all the evil behind them*—at which time, when ALL the evil they've relied upon to give them their power is in confusion—unable to give them neither the power or control they need, they will become "babbling bobbleheads" (one of my fun made-up terms)—allowing everyone to see ALL the evil, darkness, and lies behind them.

Let me give you two examples:

Back in the eighties there was a good Christian businessman being falsely accused by powerful entities that wanted to take him down. These entities had hired one of the MOST POWERFUL attorneys in the Midwest to handle this case—this attorney had *NEVER* lost a case in his two-decade plus career—he was a *POWERHOUSE* and *EVERYONE* was afraid of him.

Our friend, being a Christian—against all advice knowing who the other attorney was—only wanted to hire a Christian lawyer. He ended up choosing a shy, mousy, timid, mealy-mouthed, but super "nice-guy" Christian attorney—a GOOD Believer—but definitely NOT a powerhouse—not sure if, or how many, "wins" he had under his belt.

As memory recollects—which isn't always so perfect, especially as the years take their toll—there were four of us from our homegroup that went along with our friend that day in court.

We sat in the court gallery as hardly anyone noticed when he and his timid attorney entered.

Shortly later, the POWERHOUSE attorney entered.

There was a very noticeable PRESENCE, exuding, glowing from every part of him—his dress, his stance, his walk, his face, his looks, every part of his stone-cold demeanor—as if he had some GREAT POWER or POWERS behind him—as if some kind of "ROYALTY." He strutted around the courtroom as if he owned it. He approached the bench and as he talked to the judge you could see the judge sheepishly smiling, acknowledging him—almost cowering in submission to him—as the most powerful player in the room—and the "presumptive winner" of a "slam-dunk" case.

The case was just a formality and a waste of his precious time.

The case began with the POWERHOUSE attorney giving his opening statement—all were in *awe* as if the case was already over—and again another notch on his belt as he strutted his dominance around the courtroom. As he continued with a devilish over-confident smile radiating from his stone-cold rugged face, we began to pray—quietly, under our breath—no one could hear us at all, let alone from where we were sitting far away in the back row of the large courtroom.

We *bound and cut off* ALL the enemy in the room. We *bound and cut off* ALL the evil in and behind the POWERHOUSE attorney. We *spoke confusion, disruption, and destruction* into ALL that evil behind him.

Then something amazing happened. INSTANTLY, the Royal POWERHOUSE attorney stopped talking—*he looked stunned—he looked dazed and confused—he looked like a "lost puppy."* You could see he was trying and trying to regain his backing—trying to regain control—but could not find his bearings. Then he looked across the gallery to the back, exactly where we were sitting, as if someone or something, told him we were the cause of his problems.

He immediately asked for a side bar—requesting that the judge clear the room—the submissive judge instantly caved and cleared the room. Everyone but the prosecution and defense were escorted into the hall.

We sat there praying for the next two hours as the case was heard and eventually a judgement made.

The POWERHOUSE attorney was the first to leave the courtroom. Even though the hallway was crowded, he looked directly at us where we were sitting and scowled as he stormed by—exuding hate, anger, and disdain as *HE HAD RECEIVED THE FIRST LOSS of HIS UNTARNISHED CAREER*—even in front of and by a judge that was in his pocket.

I guess the lesson to learn here is that even the not-so-capable, timid, mealy-mouthed Christian attorney, when backed by the Lord and when the enemy is stopped, can win over the POWERHOUSE and ALL the evil behind him.

Does it kind of remind you of someone else you know of?

Maybe David versus Goliath?

Nowadays, have you ever watched the current administration or leaders of government—the Liberal, Progressive, Marxist, Socialist, Communist, Globalist, Satanist, and "axis of evil" ones—in their briefings, statements, and/or speeches?

I'm not saying that every current leader is bad or backed by evil—but some or many of that ilk most definitely are.

Have you ever noticed that sometimes some of them go into confusion—becoming "babbling bobbleheads?"

This is another example of some number of Spirit-led believers *binding up and cutting off* the evil, darkness, and lies, working behind these folks in those moments. By *SPEAKING FORTH and RELEASING*, "In the Name of Jesus," "the Light," "the Truth," and "the Blood"—then *SPEAKING CONFUSION, DISRUPTION, and DESTRUCTION* into ALL the evil behind them.

So if that's what can happen with only a few believers STANDING nowadays what would happen if we had many, many, many more?

And with *only four believers* STANDING in the courtroom that day—what could happen in our daily lives for us, our family, our friends, our churches, our governments, our countries if forty would STAND?

How about four hundred?

How about four thousand?

How about forty thousand?

How about four hundred thousand?

How about four million believers *that learned to operate in UNISON in the Spirit* in the Anointing in God's Authority?

233

GET THE POINT YET?

Don't be part of the "so heavenly bound that you're no earthly good."

We're members of both—so handle your responsibilities in both.

Do your job!

Don't bury your head in spiritual sand.

STAND—In the Name of Jesus—making your voice heard in the heavens and on the earth.

CHAPTER TWENTY-SIX

GIDEON'S ARMIES

GOD CHOOSES GIDEON

IN JUDGES 6:11-23, WE'RE told about Gideon,

"Then the angel of the Lord came and sat under the oak that was in Ophrah, which belonged to Joash the Abiezrite as his son Gideon was beating out wheat in the wine press in order to save it from the Midianites.

The angel of the Lord appeared to him and said to him, 'The Lord is with you, O valiant warrior.' Then Gideon said to him, 'O my lord, if the Lord is with us, why then has all this happened to us? And where are all His miracles which our fathers told us about, saying, Did not the Lord bring us up from Egypt? But now the Lord has abandoned us and given us into the hand of Midian.'

The Lord looked at him and said, 'Go in this your strength and deliver Israel from the hand of Midian. Have I not sent you?' He said to Him, 'O Lord, how shall I deliver Israel? Behold, my family is the least in Manasseh, and I am the youngest in my father's house.'

But the Lord said to him, Surely I will be with you, and you shall defeat Midian *as one man*...

When Gideon saw that he was the angel of the Lord, he said, 'Alas, O Lord God! For now I have seen the angel of the Lord face to face.'

The Lord said to him, 'Peace to you, do not fear; you shall not die.'"

Then in Judges 6:33-35 it continues,

"Then all the Midianites and the Amalekites and the sons of the east assembled themselves; and they crossed over and camped in the valley of Jezreel.

So the Spirit of the Lord came upon Gideon; and he blew a trumpet, and the Abiezrites were called together to follow him. He sent messengers throughout Manasseh, and they also were called together to follow him; and he sent messengers to Asher, Zebulun, and Naphtali, and they came up to meet them.

GIDEON'S 300 MEN

Continuing on in Judges 7:1-18 it says,

"Then Jerubbaal (that is, Gideon) and all the people who were with him, rose early and camped beside the spring of Harod; and the camp of Midian was on the north side of them by the hill of Moreh in the valley.

The Lord said to Gideon, 'The *people who are with you are too many* for Me to give Midian into their hands, *for Israel would become boastful*, saying, 'My own power has delivered me.'

Now therefore come, proclaim in the hearing of the people, saying, 'Whoever is afraid and trembling, let him return and depart from Mount Gilead.'

So 22,000 people returned, but **10,000 remained**.

Then the Lord said to Gideon, 'The **people are still too many**; bring them down to the water and ***I will test them for you there***. Therefore it shall be that he of whom I say to you, '*This one shall go with you, he shall go with you*; but everyone of whom I say to you, *This one shall not go with you, he shall not go.*

So he brought the people down to the water. And the Lord said to Gideon, 'You shall **separate everyone who laps the water with his tongue as a dog laps**, as well as everyone who kneels to drink.'

Now the **number of those who lapped**, putting their hand to their mouth, **was 300 men**; but all the rest of the people kneeled to drink water.

The Lord said to Gideon, '***I will deliver you with the 300 men who lapped*** and will give the Midianites into your hands; so *let all the other people go*, each man to his home'...

Now the Midianites and the Amalekites and all the sons of the east were lying in the valley as **numerous as locusts**; and *their camels were without number*, as *numerous as the sand on the seashore...*

When Gideon came, behold, a man was relating a dream to his friend... 'This is nothing less than the sword of Gideon the son of Joash, a man of Israel; God has given Midian and all the camp into his hand.'

When Gideon heard the account of the dream and its interpretation, he bowed in worship. He returned to the camp of Israel and said, 'Arise, for the Lord has given the camp of Midian into your hands.'

He divided the 300 men into three companies, and he put trumpets and empty pitchers into the hands of all of them, with torches inside the pitchers. He said to them, '***Look at me and do likewise***. And behold, when I come to the outskirts of the camp, ***do as I do***.

When I and all who are with me blow the trumpet, then you also blow the trumpets all around the camp and say, 'For the Lord and for Gideon.'"

CONFUSION OF THE ENEMY

So Gideon and the hundred men who were with him came to the outskirts of the camp at the beginning of the middle watch, when they had just posted the watch; and they blew the trumpets and smashed the pitchers that were in their hands.

When the three companies blew the trumpets and broke the pitchers, they held the torches in their left hands and the trumpets in their right hands for blowing, and cried, 'A sword for the Lord and for Gideon!'

Each **STOOD** *in his place* around the camp; *and all the army ran*, crying out as they fled.

When they blew 300 trumpets, the Lord set the sword of one against another even throughout the whole army; and the army fled as far as Beth-shittah toward Zererah, as far as the edge of Abel-meholah, by Tabbath.

THEN GOD ALLOWS THE REST OF ISRAEL TO JOIN IN

[Then, and only, then] the men of Israel were summoned from Naphtali and Asher and all Manasseh, and they pursued Midian.

Gideon sent messengers throughout all the hill country of Ephraim, saying, 'Come down against Midian and take the waters before them, as far as Beth-barah and the Jordan.' So all the men of Ephraim were summoned and they took the waters as far as Beth-barah and the Jordan.

ISRAEL IS JEALOUS

Continuing on in Judges 8:1-4, 10 it says,

"Then the men of Ephraim said to him, 'What is this thing you have done to us, not calling us when you went to fight against Midian?' And they contended with him vigorously. But he said to them, 'What have I done now in comparison with you? Is not the gleaning of the grapes of Ephraim better than the vintage of Abiezer?

God has given the leaders of Midian, Oreb and Zeeb into your hands; and what was I able to do in comparison with you?'

Then their anger toward him subsided when he said that.

Then **Gideon and the 300 men** who were with him came to the Jordan and crossed over, **weary yet pursuing**."

Now Zebah and Zalmunna were in Karkor, and their armies with them, about 15,000 men, **all who were left** of the entire army of the sons of the east; for **the fallen were 120,000 swordsmen**."

FORTY YEARS OF PEACE

And finally in Judges 8:28 it says,

"So Midian was subdued before the sons of Israel, and they did not lift up their heads anymore. And the land was undisturbed for forty years in the days of Gideon."

GOD'S DOWNSIZING

Originally when Gideon called together the armies of Israel to fight Midian he had 32,000 soldiers. This number wasn't that large of an army to stand against the total 135,000 men encompassing the entire army of the sons of the east that had come against them. That was a 1 in 4.2 ratio. Not terrible, but not great.

Then God had Gideon downsize his men from 32,000 to 10,000 soldiers. That was a 1 in 13.5 ratio. Opps, getting worse.

But God said that was still too many **because in Israel's pride** they would say they had defeated their enemies.

So God said let's downsize again.

Finally, the 300. Now it was a 1 in 450 ratio.

Yup! That's how God does it.

He works with the impossible to prove who He is and that men (and women) cannot take the credit. The pride of their strength could NEVER withstand those odds.

Later He let Gideon allow the rest of (jealous) Israel come clean up the scraps.

Opps! Where's the pride in that?

God cracks me up!

NOW LET'S LOOK AT THE BEAUTIFUL SYMBOLISMS

God is a God of symbolisms. He loves His symbols and types that He continually shows us throughout the bible.

He also loves an army that's nontypical. There are many of us who can say the "right things" and "act a certain way", but that's NOT enough. He *NEVER* wants an army based in our strength or pride.

We saw how God paired down the warriors from all who enlisted to fight to the final 300. What were their differences? Was it just because they lapped up water like a dog? Or were there more?

God wants an "army of dogs"—that will do whatever He says, whenever He says, and however He says.

Let's look at the beautiful symbols here with Gideon's Army.

First, let's look at water. Water is one of the many symbols for the Spirit of God—remember Jesus telling us that "rivers of living water would come out of us—and this He spoke of the Spirit."

So with that in mind. When we drink water it's a symbol for drinking in the Spirit of God. We all need to drink water to live in the physical realm—therefore we all need to drink in the Spirit to live in the spiritual realm.

So what's the difference with the 300 versus the others that drank from the same river?

These thirsted after the Spirit with such desperation that **they prostrated themselves** on the ground by the river **and lapped Him in**.

So that's the **number one thing** *someone must do* to be in Gideon's Armies.

Next, let's talk trumpets. The trumpet has always been used as a symbol for sounding, calling forth, and speaking forth the coming Word of the Lord.

From Joel 2:1,

"Blow the trumpet in Zion; sound an alarm on My holy Mount. Let all the inhabitants of the land tremble, for the day of [the judgment of] the Lord is coming; it is close at hand."

To Joel 2:15,

"Blow a trumpet in Zion, Consecrate a fast, proclaim a solemn assembly"

To Matthew 24:31,

"And He will send out His angels with a loud trumpet call, and they will gather His elect (His chosen ones) from the four winds, [even] from one end of the universe to the other."

When Gideon's Army blew the trumpets they were sounding forth the Current Word of the Living God.

So having the Current Word of the Living God is the **second thing** *someone must have* to be in Gideon's Armies.

Next, let's look at the earthen jar. In Second Corinthians 4:7 (NIV) it says,

"But we have this treasure in jars of clay to show that this all-surpassing Power is from God and not from us." In the NASB it says, "we have this treasure in earthen vessels." Therefore, our bodies are the jars of clay—the earthen vessels.

Next, let's talk the torches of fire inside the earthen jars. Those torches represent the Light. We've discussed Light. It's the Light of Christ [the ANOINTING] being part of the Fullness of God in the Name of Jesus. That Light is to be *FULLY ON* inside us—inside the earthen jars.

Let's look at the same verse above in context with the verse before in the AMP version to give us a broader view of how the Greek words can expand our understanding.

So Second Corinthians 4:6-7 (AMP) reads,

"For God who said, Let Light shine out of darkness, has **shone in our hearts** so as [**to beam forth**] the **Light** for the illumination of the knowledge of the majesty and glory of God [as it is manifest in the Person and is revealed] in the face of Jesus Christ (the ANOINTING).

However, we possess *this* **precious treasure** [*the* **Divine Light** *of the Gospel*] in [*frail, human*] **vessels of earth**, that the grandeur and exceeding greatness of the Power may be shown to be from God and not from ourselves."

Isn't that beautiful!

The Fullness of the Godhead, in the Light, can shine through all our puniness, feebleness, frailties, weaknesses, infirmities, and failures of our earthen jars to beam that Fullness to the world.

AMAZING!

So having that Light shining through us is the ***third thing*** *someone must have* to be in Gideon's Armies.

NOW, LET'S PUT IT ALL TOGETHER

Here are the steps to be in Gideon's Army.

Step #1: They must *lap up the Spirit of God* like they mean it.

Step #2: They must *BELIEVE and obey* God even when the odds are against them—which is REAL TRUE FAITH.

Step #3: They must *go* (spiritually) into the enemy's territory *and wait* until receiving God's direction—giving them the timing and "go ahead".

Step #4: *Sounding* the Trumpet, *the Current Word of the Living God* against their enemies.

And finally, Step #5: Then *breaking* their own earthen vessels to let the Light of Christ shine forward—*by Yielding and Choice.*

This is the army that God is looking for—*not* just *talkers*—*no pride* in themselves—*doers* according to His Word—*yielded BELIEVERS*—*choosing* Him over all else.

WHY GIDEON'S ARMIES (PLURAL) VS GIDEON'S ARMY (SINGULAR)?

Gideon only had one army (in the end) consisting of 300 dedicated warriors. Since Gideon only had one, then why do I talk about multiple armies?

Simply because we need God to raise up multiple such armies that will take their turns *STANDING* in each moment of each day, according to and directed by the Spirit of God.

It doesn't matter if for that moment it's an army of 3 or an army of 30 or an army of 300 or an army of 3,000. As long as, they're listening and obeying the Spirit of God in that moment and are cut from the same cloth.

May all who have ears to hear, come forward, and let the Lord cut you from the same cloth!

Rise up Gideon's Warriors!

CHAPTER TWENTY-SEVEN

WARNINGS FOR THE FUTURE

FALSE CHRISTS AND FALSE PROPHETS

A S DISCUSSED PREVIOUSLY, WATCH out for false Christs, false prophets, wolves in sheep's clothing, and charlatans.

Since this subject is so important. I will reiterate it again—concerning the future.

WATCH OUT FOR FALSE CHRISTS

Remember, the word *Christ* is *anointing*.

So, when you replace *Christs* with *anointings*, then it becomes much easier to understand to watch out for *false anointings*. They're out there to deceive the many and even the elect if possible.

WATCH OUT FOR FALSE PROPHETS

Remember, *false prophets speak forth from false anointings.*

As we saw in Ezekiel,

"This is what the Sovereign Lord says: WOE to the FOOLISH PROPHETS who follow their OWN SPIRIT and HAVE SEEN NOTHING!

Their VISIONS are FALSE and their DIVINATIONS a LIE.

Even though the LORD has NOT sent them, they say, 'THE LORD DECLARES.'"

Remember, false prophets include wolves in sheep's clothing and charlatans. They just come from different angles.

THE NEXT GREAT MOVE OF GOD

So now, let's talk about the next great move of God.

God's next great movement will be coming sooner than later. In case you've noticed, it's already begun. As mentioned earlier, it was already seen in two college campus revivals in early 2023—Asbury College and Texas A&M.

Would you like to see it?

Would you like to see it last?

Then pay attention, if you don't want to see it die like the previous Charismatic movement.

FIRST, PEOPLE MUST NOT FALL INTO THE MANY TRAPS

This is just a reminder since we've discussed those traps over and over to this point.

SECOND, THEY MUST GET OUT OF GOD'S WAY

Unfortunately, many won't.

THIRD, WATCH OUT FOR POWER-HUNGRY LEADERS

Those who love power and control therefore will try to take over the movement and eventually try to define it as new denominations.

WHAT'S APE+?

Leftovers from the Pentecostal and Charismatic movements of the past including many "spirit-filled" churches of today push APE+.

It stands for "A" apostle, "P" prophet, "E" evangelist, and "+" is for pastors and teachers—in total, what's called the fivefold ministry.

Ephesians 4:11–16 says,

"And, He gave some as apostles, and some as prophets, and some as evangelists, and some as pastors and teachers,

For the EQUIPPING of the saints, for the work of service,

To the BUILDING UP of the Body of Christ;

UNTIL WE ALL ATTAIN to the unity of the faith,

And, of the knowledge of the Son of God, to a mature man, to the measure of the stature which belongs to the Fullness of Christ.

From whom the whole Body, being fitted and held together, by what EVERY JOINT SUPPLIES,

According to the PROPER WORKING of EACH INDIVIDUAL PART."

We could spend hours dissecting the nuances in this scripture, but this is not the time or place, so we'll hit a few highlights.

The positions of apostles, prophets, evangelists, pastors, and teachers are still valid today. Yet some others use their interpretation of scriptures to justify their belief that APE+ went away with the early apostles in Jesus's time—but that's incorrect.

Those who recognize APE+ in God's Word think of them as the top of the pyramid in leadership and power. Dick and I would joke that "APEs" were just knuckle draggers, thinking they were "all that" and "the kings of the jungle."

VIEWED AS A PYRAMID

Let's look at the normal interpretation of church structure when viewed as a pyramid.

First, at the very top are the apostles, prophets, evangelists, pastors, and teachers. Next layer down are the elders. The next layer down are the deacons. Then at the bottom of the pyramid are the people (the peons), the sheep, the believers, the saints.

But even among the fivefold, at the top, there's a hierarchy. Apostles are at the very top of the top. Next level down are the prophets then the evangelists then the pastors and teachers.

The Western world view of the church has always been a top-down pyramid approach.

Many leaders, not all, "lust" after the APE+ positions. They'd never admit to such. They'd cloak it under the guise of "spirituality" and "pretend humility", but it's BS. It's all about their egos.

Nevertheless, it should not be so in God's Church.

Philippians 2:3–8 tells us,

"DO NOTHING from FACTIONAL MOTIVES [through contentiousness, strife, selfishness, or for unworthy ends],

Or PROMPTED by CONCEIT and EMPTY ARROGANCE.

Instead, in the TRUE SPIRIT of HUMILITY (lowliness of mind)

Let EACH REGARD the OTHERS as BETTER THAN and SUPERIOR to HIMSELF [thinking more highly of one another than you do of yourselves].

Let each of you esteem and look upon and be concerned for not [merely] his own interests, but also each for the interests of others.

Let this SAME ATTITUDE and PURPOSE and [HUMBLE] MIND be in YOU which was in Christ Jesus: [let HIM be YOUR EXAMPLE in HUMILITY:]

Who, although being essentially one with God and in the form of God [possessing the Fullness of the attributes which make God God],

Did not think this equality with God was a thing to be eagerly grasped or retained,

But STRIPPED HIMSELF [of ALL PRIVILEGES and RIGHTFUL DIGNITY],

So as to ASSUME the GUISE of a SERVANT (slave), in that He became like men and was born a human being.

He ABASED and HUMBLED HIMSELF [still further] and CARRIED HIS OBEDIENCE to the EXTREME ofF DEATH, even the death of the cross!"

NOW LET'S TALK GOD'S TRUTH

It will not be the Western world's interpretation of power—not close.

God's Truth is that the "normal" view is entirely, wholly, absolutely wrong.

It's backward.

You say, "What?"

Yeah, backward.

Instead of a top-down pyramid, God's Truth is an upside-down pyramid—bottom on top—where the least are the greatest and the greatest are the least.

Jesus said,

"The one WHO is the GREATEST AMONG YOU must BECOME like the YOUNGEST [LEAST],

And the LEADER like the SERVANT.

For who is greater, the one who reclines at the table or the one who serves? Is it not the one who reclines at the table?

But I AM AMONG YOU as the ONE WHO SERVES." (Luke 22:26)

In an upside-down pyramid, the people (the peons), the sheep, the believers, the saints are at the top. Next level down are the deacons. The next level down are the elders. At the very bottom are the fivefold—and in their layer, the pastors and teachers are next, then the evangelists, then the prophets, and at the very bottom of the bottom are the apostles.

OOPS!

That view would mess up a bunch of power-hungry, ego-controlled, wannabe leaders.

They don't get to be on top.

Instead, they get to be on the very bottom of the bottom, servant to all.

Not the Western world's view—probably not their view.

I'm sure they'd tell you I'm crazy and have no idea what I'm talking about.

Yup, that's because they actually love the Western world's view of power in the church.

Remember, people love power.

It's a major flaw the ruler of this world knows all too well—and has used and continues to use—to seduce many to fail, even the elect, if possible.

As the old saying goes,

"Power corrupts, and absolute power corrupts absolutely." (Lord Acton, nineteenth-century British politician)

WHY UPSIDE DOWN?

So, why do I say the pyramid is upside down?

God calls all leaders, including the fivefold, to *undergird* the people and *overseer* them, not to be overlords.

In Second Corinthians 1:24, we're told,

"Not that we LORD it over YOUR FAITH,

But we are WORKERS with YOU for YOUR JOY, because it is by faith you Stand firm."

It's actually in the same original scripture, Ephesians 4, that clearly tells us what the APE+ positions are to be—let's look back at it.

It states,

"For the EQUIPPING of the SAINTS, for the work of service,

To the BUILDING UP, of the BODY of Christ;

UNTIL, we all attain to the unity of the faith."

So, what does that mean?

ALL these leaders have been tasked by the Lord to do three things:

First, *EQUIP* the saints.

Second, *BUILDUP* the Body of Christ.

And third, *UNTIL*—yes, UNTIL, not for ever, only, UNTIL—UNTIL we attain to the unity of the faith.

When we attain that teaching, training, and infusion of CHRIST (the ANOINTING), we're to be released to do the jobs—whatever functions the Lord would have us do.

The people (the peons), the sheep, the believers, the saints are the ones at the top, who are supposed to do the work. We've been given the task to carry the ANOINTING into the world through our everyday lives.

So, contrary to Western world's leadership interpretations, the leaders are at the bottom.

Yes, in the beginning and along the path, *their job is to oversee and help protect the sheep*; but more importantly, they're to *undergird the people* and *raise them up*, building up the Body of Christ.

UNTIL, AND ONLY, UNTIL

Therefore, their job is an "UNTIL ministry."

Note: Some still wanting to retain power will argue that "attaining to the unity of the faith" is a *lifetime process.* Therefore, their job (and power and control) will *NEVER* be done.

FALSE.

The fivefold must position themselves at, the bottom of the bottom, to support the saints, to lift (build) them up, and *do EVERYTHING possible to WORK THEMSELVES OUT of a JOB.*

Then they are *functioning IN CHRIST.*

If not, then they're *operating under false Christs and false anointings,* in turn making them *false apostles and false prophets.*

WORD TO THE WISE

Never think to highly of apostles and prophets. Never fall under such deception. Never love (or worship) "Apostle so and so" or "Prophet this and that."

At BEST, they are *unworthy servants who did their job;* and for that, their reward is before the Father in Heaven, someday—not now, not here.

How do I know the Western world's interpretation of leadership and the error of their ways?

I've watched many, and before gaining understanding, I wanted to be one of them too.

But the Father loved me too much and, instead, humbled me.

He graciously didn't let me become one of them, and now, only fifty-plus years later, am I allowed to talk about all this.

THE WARNING FOR THE UPCOMING NEXT GREAT MOVE OF GOD

Leaders and people of God: Do not repeat the same mistakes of the past.

If you want to see the Power and Anointing of God manifest without ALL the other crap, then

GET OUT OF THE WAY—ALL OF YOU.

Otherwise, you're doomed to repeat the same mistakes over and over—*and KILL the MOVE, again.*

You'll just end up operating like the Seven Sons of Sceva with *NO AUTHORITY* or just fall into one of the devil's many other traps. *Not forgetting that one of the worst traps is to LOVE POWER too much and then misuse it.*

Or *thinking YOU'RE in CHARGE of the MOVE*—or *IT'S YOUR JOB to "RUN" or "CONTROL" it*—or *fall under the HORRIBLE MISCONCEPTION that YOU HAD ANYTHING to do WITH IT.*

WAY OFF?

You may think I'm way off talking about this in a spiritual warfare manual—but actually, I'm NOT.

Because if you don't understand the fundamentals of God's Power, how to YIELD to it, NOT try to CONTROL it, then you're doomed to repeat the same failures over and over and over.

Unless we cry and weep, wanting, praying, yielding for change from the old, we're doomed to fail again and again and again.

You may think I'm on a tangent or I digress.

You might be right, but maybe not.

CHAPTER TWENTY-EIGHT

REJECT...

AGAIN, FROM THE NEGATIVE VIEWPOINT

I N LIGHT OF ALL stated to this point in time, and knowing that I'm repeating myself again, I will restate these things from a clear concise NEGATIVE VIEWPOINT of REJECTION.

REJECT FALSE CHRISTS

When you replace the word *Christ* with *anointing*, then it becomes much easier to understand.

Therefore, *REJECT false anointings.*

REJECT FALSE APOSTLES AND FALSE PROPHETS

False apostles and false prophets are based in and promoted by *false anointings.*

Therefore, *REJECT them.*

Also, *reject* wolves in sheep's clothing and charlatans *as false prophets in disguise.*

REJECT MEN OR WOMEN WHO WANT POWER AND CONTROL

People who think they are, or others exclaim as, "God's gift."

They're NOT.

That's just a bunch of BS.

Just because God gives gifts to men and women doesn't mean they're something special or deserve it.

On one hand, God gives gifts to ALL His people.

"Now there are varieties of gifts, but the same SPIRIT.

And there are varieties of ministries, and the same LORD.

There are varieties of effects, but the same God who works ALL things in ALL persons.

But to EACH ONE is GIVEN the MANIFESTATION of the SPIRIT for the common good.

For to one, is given the word of wisdom, through the SPIRIT,

And to another, the word of knowledge, according to the same SPIRIT;

To another, faith, by the same SPIRIT,

And to another, gifts of healing, by the same SPIRIT,

And to another, the effecting of miracles,

And to another, prophecy,

And to another, the distinguishing of spirits,

To another, various kinds of tongues,

And to another, the interpretation of tongues.

But one and the same SPIRIT, works all these things,

Distributing to EACH ONE, INDIVIDUALLY, just as He wills." (1 Corinthians 12:4–11)

And Romans 11:29 says,

"For GOD'S GIFTS, and HIS CALL, are IRREVOCABLE.

He never withdraws them when once they are given,

And, He does not change His mind about those to whom He gives His Grace, or to whom He sends His call."

WHAT DOES IT MEAN THAT GOD'S GIFTS ARE IRREVOCABLE?

It means they're binding.

Irreversible.

Final.

Unalterable.

Unchangeable.

"He never withdraws them when once they are given."

But, isn't this just another one of God's NEGATIVE statements again?

Why would someone say they're "irrevocable?"

Does that mean that maybe, in some, or many cases, they should be revoked?

YES.

If it depended upon us and our "good works," they should.

Knowing this, never magnify people or gifts.

People don't have the gifts because they're "special."

They have them because God gave them, and He never took them away no matter what, even if they began to listen, follow, and function out of the wrong (false) anointings.

Therefore, never think too highly of people or their gifts.

AND, FINALLY, REJECT ALL EVIL

You can do this by *learning to STAND every day* "In the Name of Jesus" and *by speaking forth and releasing* "the Light," "the Truth," and "the Blood."

CHAPTER TWENTY-NINE

YOUR ONE AND ONLY FREEBEE

SPOILER ALERT: THIS CHAPTER IS HERE BECAUSE I KNOW SOME PEOPLE NEED TO JUMP TO THE END, FIRST

NUMEROUS PEOPLE HAVE ASKED how to pray the STAND, and as I've said before, I REFUSE to give EXACT WORDS so that it DOES NOT BECOME ROTE. I've also emphasized throughout that you need to learn these things before the Lord, as you study the manual, so that He makes them "yours."

In addition, as you would've learned in this manual by this point, that if you DO NOT WALK with THE LORD and in HIS AUTHORITY, you will get your ass handed to you by the devil—and that would be the nicest thing that might happen—it could be much worse.

BUT I WILL GIVE YOU A "FREEBEE"

The following are a few bullet points for a *BASIC STAND that ALL BELIEVERS CAN DO* before receiving FULL training (from the manual) on HOW-TO WALK-IN AUTHORITY—which is a MUST for (even) BELIEVERS—or they too will get the $hit beat out of them like the Seven Sons of Sceva.

First, *you must be a believer* who has received the Lord Jesus Christ into your heart and life.

Second, *always yield your heart and mind* to the Lord before doing the STAND.

Third, then *you can say and proclaim* before the heavens and the earth:

"In the Name of Jesus, I agree with and thereby release the Light, the Truth, and the Blood."

Because the Light EXPOSES and DISPELS ALL DARKNESS—the Truth EXPOSES and DISPELS ALL LIES (including ALL propaganda and gaslighting)—and the Blood PROTECTS ALL BELIEVERS and TAKES OUT ALL EVIL.

This very simple statement will have IMMEASURABLE POSITIVE EFFECTS.

Therefore, you can say and proclaim it *as often as you want* and *into any situation*, as long as, IT'S NOT ROTE and YOU MEAN IT from a YIELDED HEART. The rest of the STAND will come after you've learned it from the manual.

FOR ONE REASON AND ONE REASON ONLY

The only reason I'm giving you this "freebee" here and now is because we need MULTITUDES of believers to LEARN and STAND (ASAP)—whether BASIC or FULL—especially in these perilous end times—for ALL of our lives to be with the Lord, for protections, for healings, and to change the Church and the world.

NOW IT'S UP TO YOU.

ABOUT THE AUTHOR

HI, I'M TOM SNOW

First, let me introduce myself:

I'm a conservative Believer and not part of any organized religion or denomination. As a Jewish Christian I believe that there is one God who created all and all are equal in God's creation. That there is only one True Church which is the Body of Christ ~ of which All True Believers are a part. I believe in God's Light that dispels darkness and binarily separates Truth from lies. I believe we not only have spiritual responsibility in the Church, but also equally in the world.

In fifty-plus years I've been tested in many ways, gone to hell and back, and lived to tell about it. Walking with the Lord is *SIMPLE*, it's just not *EASY*. The road is narrow. These works are a result of being humbled and learning over those many years, and still learning today, tomorrow, and until His return. My goal is to share what little I've learned along the way to help equip other Believers to learn to Walk in the Anointing, then Stand in God's Authority.

While many are chasing a million different answers in a million different ways, there's only *ONE*. ALL the Greatest Mysteries, Wisdom, Understandings, and Secrets of God and the Universe are revealed inside *ONE Simple Truth: being IN CHRIST*. Hence, I want to live my life in the Presence and the Heart of the Father, Papa God.

Second, here's what I've done:

I'm the owner of a software design company—and have been in hardware and software design for over forty-five years. I'm an engineer, inventor, entrepreneur, and fisherman; but most importantly, I love the Lord, my beautiful wife, my five children, and my eight grandchildren.

And, nowadays, I'm writing books as the Lord directs.

Made in the USA
Columbia, SC
30 November 2024

47944519R00150